What Jesus Said and Why It Matters Now

TIMOTHY D. FALLON

ST. ANTHONY MESSENGER PRESS

Cincinnati, Ohio

Scripture passages have been taken from *New Revised Standard Version Bible*, copyright ©1989 by the Division of Christian Education of the National Council of the Churches of Christ in the U.S.A., and used by permission. All rights reserved.

Cover and book design by Mark Sullivan.
Cover photos from www.istockphoto.com.
Photographers: Suzanne Long/Long Shot Photography (top); Giulio Pons (bottom).

Library of Congress Cataloging-in-Publication Data

Fallon, Timothy D.
  What Jesus said and why it matters now / Timothy D. Fallon.
    p. cm.
  Includes bibliographical references (p. 133).
  ISBN 0-86716-673-8 (pbk. : alk. paper) 1. Christian life–Biblical teaching. 2. Bible. N.T.
Gospels–Criticism, interpretation, etc. I. Title.

BS2555.6.C48F35 2006
226'.06–dc22

                                                                2006025977

ISBN-13 978-0-86716-673-6
ISBN-10 0-86716-673-8
Copyright ©2006 Timothy D. Fallon. All rights reserved.

Published by St. Anthony Messenger Press
28 W. Liberty St.
Cincinnati, OH 45202
www.AmericanCatholic.org

Printed in the United States of America

Printed on acid-free paper

06 07 08 09 10 5 4 3 2 1

To my grandchildren—Alex, Sarah, Rachel, Danielle, Jared and Joshua—with my prayer that you will grow to love God's word

CONTENTS

ACKNOWLEDGMENTS

Even a simple book such as this one has a huge supporting cast. My heartfelt thanks to the many people who helped make this book possible. I'm grateful to my wife, Carla, for understanding my need to write this book, being patient with the time it took and providing valuable feedback at various stages of the manuscript. Special thanks to my lifelong friend Tim McGuire for his editorial expertise, his candid though sometimes brutal feedback and his loving support. The finished work is vastly improved because of him. I owe a debt of gratitude to Father John Young; the many retreats we led together were my first experiences of personalizing the Gospels. Thanks to those who read early chapters and provided feedback and encouragement: Pat Sweeney, Midge Sweeney, Jill Edelen, Ted Anspaugh, Carol Anspaugh, Tom Giardino, S.M., and Holly Rosenhagen. I am grateful to two longtime friends and ministry colleagues—Marisa Guerin and Tom Zanzig—for encouraging my writing and helping me find a publisher. Thanks to Father Larry Shinnick for his help and to Father Al McBride, O.P., for his gracious response to my questions about publishing. I appreciate Trevah Dalrymple's help with preparing the manuscript. Finally, a "bless you" to the people at St. Anthony Messenger Press—including Lisa Biedenbach, Mary Curran Hackett and Abby Colich. Thanks for taking a chance on an unpublished author and for your patience guiding me through the process.

INTRODUCTION

When my grandson Alex chooses a bedtime story for me to read, he usually picks the longest one he can find. Like most kids, he will do whatever he can to put off going to bed. There is, however, a more important reason: He loves stories, and he wants the experience to last.

Like Alex, I love stories too. A movie grabs me, and I am transported to another time and place. My own life is left behind, and I embark on an adventure. When I am absorbed in the pages of a novel, I wrestle with the same struggles as the characters—laughing, crying, winning, losing, grieving, celebrating and cheering them on.

Stories are so much a part of us that we are drawn to listening to them and telling them. I remember one family reunion when my Uncle Leo captivated us by telling stories of growing up on the farm. My favorite was the time he and a friend made a parachute and tied a basket to it. Then, they put a cat in the basket and dropped it from the barn loft. Fortunately, the cat landed safely. (It may, however, have only had eight lives left.) Leo and his friend weren't so lucky. When my grandpa found out about the feline paratrooper, they won an all-expenses-paid trip to the woodshed.

A good story touches us deeply, evokes a powerful emotional response and moves us at a profound level.

The purpose of this book is to help you personalize the stories in the Gospels—and to help find meaning in what Jesus did and said, and explore why it matters to you *now*. We personalize a Gospel story by entering into its conflict, experiencing its energy and emotion and letting it absorb us. When we connect with the story at this experiential level, it reveals something of our deepest longings and our ultimate hopes. We begin to recognize the ways in which an incarnate God is touching us. Personalizing the stories of the Gospels invites us into the

Jesus experience, calls us to a deeper understanding of our identity in God and urges us to live out that identity in our everyday lives.

I first learned about personalizing Gospel stories while conducting retreats for high school students. During these retreats I would encourage the participants to dramatize Gospel stories to help them grasp their meaning. On one such retreat I was helping a group prepare to role-play the story of Jesus being lost in the temple (Luke 2:41–52). We were talking about all the things that Jesus experienced: wondering about his purpose in life, needing a chance to explore who he was, getting into hassles with his parents, trying to understand his relationship with God. The central conflict in this story is that when Mary and Joseph leave Jerusalem, Jesus stays behind without asking permission. His parents search frantically for three days before they find him. One young man captured the essence of this conflict and exclaimed: "If I pulled a stunt like that, I'd be grounded for life!" At that moment he had personalized the story. He had grasped the experience of Jesus and his parents and recognized how his own experience was similar to theirs.

This book focuses on helping you personalize seven Gospel stories. Its structure is quite simple. This introduction explains what it means to personalize a Gospel story and provides suggestions for how to read the book. The next seven chapters are "story chapters." Each one helps you personalize a specific Gospel story. The last chapter, which can be read at any time, explains a method for personalizing Gospel stories. By outlining this method, I hope to encourage you to deepen your ability to make Gospel stories your own and to use that ability with stories not in this book.

The stories that I have selected for this book are the Gospels proclaimed during the seasons of Lent and Easter in the Catholic church—as well as in other Christian traditions that follow the same lectionary. The lectionary follows a three-year cycle, and I have selected Year A. The story chapters have a particular relevance for catechumens and candidates in the Rite of Christian Initiation of Adults (RCIA) because they focus on Gospel stories used for "breaking open the word" during the Sundays of Lent. As a result, this book is an excellent resource for anyone involved in the RCIA—catechumens, candidates, sponsors and team members.

Each story chapter is structured the same way—based on three fundamental questions that are at the heart of personalizing the gospel.

- *What's the experience of the story?* This section of each chapter sets the scene to help you put the story in context, and it provides the scriptural reference for the story so that you can read "the original" version. It also retells the story in an engaging way to help you enter into the experience of the story.

- *How does this story touch me?* The second section draws key themes out of the experience of the story. For each theme, it juxtaposes the experiences of the people in the Gospel story with experiences in contemporary life. Sometimes these are my own experiences. Other times they are the experiences of others—including scenes from movies or literature. As these experiences touch you, you will recognize how your own experiences are similar to the people in the story and begin to make the Gospel your own story.

- *How does this story call me to live?* This section will help you "take the story with you" during your day and week. It includes questions to help you continue to reflect on the story and a suggestion for using the story to enter into prayer.

As you read each chapter, I suggest that you keep in mind a litmus test to gauge whether you have personalized the story—boredom. When I succeed in personalizing a story, I am never bored. I may be beside myself with worry and fear—as Mary and Joseph were when they were looking for their lost son in Jerusalem (Luke 2:41–52). I may be angry, like the vineyard workers who had toiled though the heat of the day and thought they deserved more pay than those who arrived at the eleventh hour (Matthew 20:1–16). I may be stricken with grief and as disillusioned as Martha and Mary were when Jesus failed to arrive until after Lazarus died (John 11:1–46). I may be overcome with joy and run to tell others, like the disciples on the road to Emmaus were when they recognized Jesus in the breaking of the bread (Luke 24:13–35). I may feel all of this and more, but I am never bored.

My grandson Alex hates boredom. When it comes to Gospel stories, I hate boredom too. I hope this book will help you experience Gospel stories in a new way, engage in them at the personal level and discover the ways that God touches you. As you begin this book, my prayer is that you will have the courage to enter into these stories and let them speak. If you embrace each story as a spiritual adventure and surrender to it, it will pass the litmus test. You will not be bored. In fact, you may never be the same.

CHAPTER ONE

CLAIMING OUR TRUE IDENTITY

Jesus Is Tempted in the Desert (Matthew 4:1–17)

WHAT'S THE EXPERIENCE OF THE STORY?

Setting the Scene

Jesus' temptation in the desert occurs at a pivotal moment in his life. His time of preparation has ended, and he is about to take up his public ministry. Jesus leaves the safety of Galilee, seeks out John on the banks of the Jordan and convinces John to baptize him.

For Jesus, baptism is a profound encounter with God that deepens his understanding of his identity as God's beloved Son. Now, in the wilderness, he is tested about the true meaning of that identity. He is on the threshold of his ministry, and the stakes are high. John is about to be imprisoned and executed. Jesus knows enough about the prophets to be aware of the danger he is facing. John's arrest leaves little doubt that some of those in authority will be threatened by his message. They will do whatever is necessary to maintain their positions of power.

Jesus is led into the desert to complete his preparation. The wilderness is a dangerous place—a place of climate extremes, a place where thieves and outcasts take refuge, a place where animals stalk their prey. In the wilderness Jesus is forced to confront his fears and wrestle with the true nature of his identity and mission.

Reading the Gospel

Read Matthew's account of Jesus' temptation in the desert: Matthew 4:1–17.

Retelling the Story

This story begins with a surprise: It is the Spirit that leads Jesus into the wilderness. Our tendency is to envision God as keeping us safe rather than putting us in harm's way. Yet the Spirit now takes Jesus to a dangerous place he didn't choose. In the wilderness he will be subjected to severe tests, and he will either succeed or fail.

Curiously, Satan begins the first two temptations with the same phrase: "If you are the Son of God..." (vv. 3, 5). What's at stake in these temptations is what it means to be God's Son. The temptations help reveal the true nature of Jesus' identity. Satan makes no attempt to convince Jesus that he isn't God's Son, but the tempter tries to seduce Jesus into understanding that identity in ways that are contrary to his mission. The challenge Jesus faces is grasping the true meaning of his identity and making his relationship with God the central focus of his life. If he gives in to temptation, he will live in a way that is contrary to being the beloved Son, use his power for self-serving purposes and—ultimately—align himself with the forces of evil.

THE FIRST TEMPTATION: WHAT IS THE FOCUS OF JESUS' LONGING?
After forty days of fasting, Jesus is famished. The tempter tries to exploit this need with a helpful suggestion. Expanding slightly on Matthew's brief account, I imagine the tempter's argument going something like this: "Of course you're hungry. After so many days of fasting and prayer, who wouldn't be? If you're God's Son, why not just command these stones to become loaves of bread? After all, this ministry is going to be difficult, and you'll need your strength. Do you really think that God wants his beloved to walk around hungry? You deserve something to eat. Go ahead, turn the stone to bread."

Jesus' response makes clear that there is much more at stake here than physical hunger and the bread that satisfies it. He goes right to the heart of the issue. Again, if I imagine the dialogue in a slightly expanded form, Jesus' response might go something like this: "Yes, I'm hungry. The true nature of my hunger, however, has little to do with bread. God is the ultimate object of my longing. The true focus of my attention is every word that comes from God. Prayer and fasting are the ways I focus all my energy and attention—everything that I am—on God and the word of God. I am God's beloved, and only God can fulfill my longing."

Jesus grasps the essence of this temptation: where he directs his ultimate longing and how he will use his power. If he makes bread the ultimate object of his longing, he is letting his human weakness get in the way of his relationship with God. If he uses his power as God's Son to turn stones into bread, he is using that power in a self-serving way. Jesus recognizes that he has been given power to carry out his mission, not to satisfy his physical hunger.

As we personalize the first temptation, we are confronted with the realities of our humanness—hunger and thirst, vulnerability and powerlessness, fear and loneliness, ache and need. In response to this temptation, we are called to reject the self-serving uses of power and focus our longing on God and the Word of God.

THE SECOND TEMPTATION: WHERE WILL JESUS PLACE HIS ULTIMATE TRUST?

The scene of this temptation changes—perhaps in a vision or prayer—from the desert to Jerusalem. The tempter takes Jesus to the pinnacle of the temple, a place high above the holy city. Matthew again recounts a dialogue between Jesus and Satan that focuses on what it means to be the Son of God. The tempter quotes Scripture to suggest that Jesus throw himself down from the temple. His argument is that because Jesus is God's beloved Son, God will send angels to prevent him from being harmed. Jesus responds by saying that he will not put God to the test.

There is a way in which this temptation seems almost humorous. Satan suggests that Jesus force God to make a diving catch by throwing himself off the temple. We've all been tempted to ask God for diving catches, heroic rescues that keep us safe in spite of ourselves. Two fundamental questions that Jesus wrestles with throughout his life are at the heart of this temptation. The first is whether he will fully accept the reality of being human. The second is whether he will put his total trust in God.

Will Jesus accept the full reality of being human? Being human involves experiencing suffering, feeling the full range of positive and negative emotions, confronting limitations and coping with uncertainty and vulnerability. To be true to his identity as God's beloved, Jesus must embrace all of this. Only by opening himself to the full range of human experience can Jesus be the authentic son of a compassionate God that pours out love and mercy on all humankind.

In this temptation Satan is suggesting that there is an easier way. He tempts Jesus to avoid all the messy inconvenience of being human. In effect, he suggests that because Jesus is God's beloved, he can use his special relationship with God to avoid the vulnerability and suffering that come with being human. Throw yourself down from the temple and God will make a diving catch. Because you are God's special one, the law of gravity need not apply to you.

The temptation that Satan offers may seem trivial, but it's very cunning. If Jesus will avoid humanness in the desert, it sets him up for the ultimate temptation—using his special relationship with God to avoid the suffering and death of the cross. In Gethsemane Jesus will face the ultimate test of humanness: Will he stay faithful to his mission as the beloved Son of God even when the cost is suffering and death? In facing that ultimate temptation, Jesus will once again have to decide whether he will use his special relationship as God's beloved to save his skin.

When the tempter suggests that he throw himself down from the temple, Jesus' response is to quote Scripture: "Do not put the Lord your God to the test" (v. 7). In effect, Jesus' response to Satan goes something like this: "I won't throw myself down from the temple and ask God for a miracle. I know that God is with me, and I will not demand a sign. I have confidence in God, and I don't need a diving catch by angels to reassure me."

Weak faith demands signs and reassurances. Jesus' faith is strong enough to trust the quiet presence of God. It is strong enough not to put God to the test.

THE THIRD TEMPTATION: WHAT KINGDOM WILL JESUS SERVE?
The third temptation is blatantly clear. The tempter takes Jesus to a high mountain and shows him the splendor of all the kingdoms of the world. Then he offers a deal. If Jesus will fall down and worship him, Satan will give him all of these kingdoms.

Satan attempts to seduce Jesus into idolatry using wealth and power. The tempter's intent is to have Jesus turn away from God, worship him and serve earthly kingdoms. In several brief verses, this temptation portrays the cosmic battle between good and evil, God and Satan. The question at the heart of this temptation is what kingdom Jesus will serve. The first two temptations set the stage, but this is the culmination. Satan wants Jesus' heart and soul, and wealth and power are the bait he uses to close the deal.

Jesus refuses to take the bait, rejects Satan, and chooses to worship and serve God alone. His response to this temptation makes it clear that he rejects the wealth of earthly kingdoms. He chooses instead to set his heart on God and God's kingdom. Wealth all too easily gets in the way of God. At best, it has the ability to distract us from giving God our full attention. At worst, we can become so caught up in the pursuit of wealth that it supplants God as the object of our worship. By rejecting wealth, Jesus chooses the poverty of relying solely on God. That poverty requires him to open himself to God and receive everything as a gift. Because he owns nothing, Jesus has no need to spend his energy protecting his possessions. He has nothing to distract him from his relationship with God and the mission he is called to fulfill. He lives with a radical trust that God will provide whatever he needs.

Satan also tries to seduce Jesus with power, and Jesus' response is intriguing. He does not respond by refusing power. He needs power to carry out his mission. His response is to choose the life-giving, redemptive power that comes from God and to reject the oppressive, dominating power that is a defining characteristic of earthly kingdoms. Throughout his ministry Jesus uses this power to touch people in their deepest need, proclaim the radical availability of God's mercy, heal the sick and broken, forgive those imprisoned by sinful ways and urge all those who will listen to give their hearts to God. He rejects the self-serving power that flows from his ego and the desire for control.

As we personalize this story of Jesus' temptation, we are called to examine our own response to wealth and power.

HOW DOES THE STORY TOUCH ME?

As I reflect on how the story of Jesus' temptation in the desert touches my life, here are some of the ways that I connect with the experience of the story.

Experiencing the Wilderness

Like Jesus, our journey takes us to the wilderness, to a dangerous place that we haven't chosen, to a strange place we must befriend. At a critical point in my life, that wilderness was leaving home and friends behind to seek out a new life in a strange city.

I was in my mid-twenties, and my career was in full swing. To all outward appearances, life was unfolding according to plan. Something inside me, however, had a different view. I was wrestling with the troubling instinct that I wasn't ready for what lay ahead of me. It was only a matter of time before I would confront barriers I couldn't overcome. My first response was to ignore this inner warning. The cost of listening to it seemed too great. I needed time and the counsel of several close friends to find the courage to face it.

After a period of searching and questioning, I finally decided to return to school for a graduate degree. That decision meant leaving my lifelong home in Michigan and moving to California. Making that decision took more than courage; it required a leap of faith. Could I leave everything behind, find a way to make ends meet and create a new life for myself? That experience taught me something of the wilderness, what it asks of you and how it prepares you.

I have an image embedded in my memory that captures something about what entering the wilderness was like for me. The scene is my first view of San Francisco on the day I moved there. The rain was pouring down as I drove across the Bay Bridge, and the city was totally engulfed in fog. It looked as though the bridge disappeared into a cloud of gloom. There I was, surrounded by most of what I owned, driving into a city where I knew no one. I had no idea where I was going to live or even where I would spend the night. As I squinted through the windshield into the haze, the road ahead was barely visible. In that moment I learned something of how lonely the wilderness can be. I felt a deep sadness for what I had left behind, and I was frightened by what lay ahead. I couldn't explain what it was that I was trying to do or why I needed to do it. Yet I knew that I had no choice but to see it through. Somehow I had to befriend this strange place and make it my home.

Over the next several days I began to find my way around San Francisco. More importantly, I learned something about myself, the wilderness and prayer. Before leaving Michigan, my life had been busy—too busy. I knew that I needed time for solitude and prayer, but I was afraid of what they would demand of me. In the wilderness of a strange city, I committed myself to spending time in prayer every day. I'll never forget the first morning that I tried to make good on that commitment. I gathered up my Bible and my journal, and I sat down in a chair facing the window. I lit a candle to set the mood, and I sat back and took a deep breath. Within two seconds, a frightened voice inside of me shouted: "Now what do I do!"

That terrible moment—when we realize that we have no idea what to do—is the moment of surrender. By admitting that we are lost, we begin to open ourselves to silence and waiting. In such moments, prayer is born. We are no longer in control, and so we leave room for God to work. We let go of our agendas, and we listen. Henri Nouwen captured this moment of surrender beautifully with a simple image to describe prayer: with open hands.[1] When we surrender, we open our hands. We admit that we are not in control, and we listen for God's guidance in our lives.

People experience the wilderness in many ways. For Jesus the wilderness was a desert where he was exposed to the physical extremes of heat and cold, hunger and thirst, and the temptation to betray his true identity. For me, it was moving to a strange city and learning to befriend solitude and prayer. You have your own experience of the wilderness. Perhaps it was hearing that the biopsy was positive, having death rob you of a loved one, or saying "yes" to an inner imperative that you couldn't explain. We find ourselves in the wilderness whenever our fears loom large, we are exposed to our humanness and we find ourselves at risk. The wilderness is a place where we are in the grip of our emotions, and we are forced to find our way. It is the place where we confront our weaknesses and experience trials we are not sure we can endure.

When we enter the wilderness, our feet leave the diving board and we find ourselves in midair. It is the point in our prayer when we somehow find the courage to surrender, the moment in which we say "yes" to love or "no" to an addiction, the place where good and evil vie for control of our lives. It is a place of inner struggle when the voices in our heads argue about which path to take. In the wilderness, our doubts loom large, we are vulnerable and we are forced to choose. The wilderness is a continental divide in our lives where the energy flowing in one direction begins to flow in the other.

Jesus' temptation in the wilderness is fundamental to his life and essential to his ministry. It is a critical preparatory step, an intense wrestling with his identity as beloved Son of God. It is an encounter with the cosmic forces of good and evil in which he is tempted to turn away from his mission and use his relationship with God in a self-serving way. Whenever we face similar struggles, we experience the same wilderness that Jesus did. Our wilderness is that place where we are most vulnerable, most deeply aware of our humanness. It is the place where we are tempted to put things other than God at the center of our lives. It takes courage to face this wilderness. Instinctively, we know that the silence of the wilderness exposes our vulnerabilities and is easily invaded—both by our fears and by the power of God.

Claiming Our True Identity

Jesus experienced the wilderness as a place where he wrestled with the true meaning of his identity and call. Like Jesus, each of us is gifted with a marvelous uniqueness, an authentic identity in God. Finding that uniqueness and living it out is the most difficult challenge of our lives. When our humanness and vulnerability loom large, it is all too easy to settle for being less than we are called to be.

Mark graduated from college with a degree from a top-ten business school. His first job in business, however, left him frustrated and unfulfilled. He changed jobs only to find that once again he was unfulfilled. He began to question what he should do with his life. That soul-searching led him to leave his job in business and take a temporary job as a plumber. Freed from the roles that he knew weren't right for him, he was able to ask a more fundamental question: *What should I do with my life?*

After a period of considerable self-doubt and uncertainty, Mark decided to become an elementary school teacher. He returned to school with a new motivation and spent three years earning a second degree and his teaching certificate. After a successful student teaching experience and his second graduation, he summed up his experience simply: "I think I've finally found my calling."

Mark realized that he had found his calling just after his thirtieth birthday. Some of us never do. Calling goes deeper than what we do, deeper than job or even career. Calling is about who we are in God. Each of us is called to live our identity in God in some unique way. I am the only one who can live my call, and you are the only who can live yours. If either one of us fails to find and live our call, there will be a missing thread in the tapestry of life.

Jesus' desert experience helped him grasp the true nature of his call. Mark entered a similar desert by admitting that his first choice of career left him empty and unfulfilled. After wandering in that desert of self-doubt and questioning, Mark discovered that becoming an elementary teacher was his unique way of living his identity in God. Like Jesus and Mark, each of us is called to the wilderness to open ourselves to God's call. In the wilderness we discover our true identity in God and become the unique thread in the tapestry of life that only we can be.

Experiencing Temptation

Every temptation tries to prevent us from living out our unique identity in God. The temptations that Jesus faced attempted to confuse him about his true identity and the nature of his call. It is the same for us. As we try to live out our identity in God, we are confronted with significant obstacles. Like Jesus, we find ourselves wrestling with our longing, deciding where to place our ultimate trust and determining what kingdom we will serve.

WHAT IS THE FOCUS OF YOUR LONGING?

In the first temptation Jesus confronts his physical hunger, wrestles with the depth of his longing and chooses to focus his ultimate longing on God. Personalizing Jesus' first temptation requires that we wrestle with our deepest longings. Temptation gets its foothold in such human needs as hunger, loneliness, sexual longing, fear and self-doubt. It forces us to choose how we will satisfy those needs.

When I face my longings and temptations, I am not as single-minded and right-hearted as Jesus. My struggle is captured by a quote from Alfred E. Newman, the mythical founder of *MAD Magazine*: "Most people don't know what they want, but they're pretty sure that they haven't got it."[2] Throughout my life I've had an unfulfilled hunger. I have, however, often been confused about what I hungered for and how to satisfy that hunger. All too often I have lived out Newman's quote. I haven't been sure of what I wanted, but I've been pretty sure I didn't have it.

Since childhood I've had an intense need to achieve. Whatever the arena—school, extracurricular activities, career or even games and hobbies—I have always been driven to excel. Some powerful hunger in me fueled this need, and it took me years to understand this hunger enough to keep it from controlling my life. I grew up as the second son of high-achieving parents. Some of my earliest memories involve competing with my brother who was nearly three years older. When he learned to ride a bicycle, I learned to ride one too—so that he wouldn't leave me behind. When he started playing baseball, I started too. Even though our age gap left me significantly disadvantaged, I always wanted to beat him. That desire to win was a strong element of my childhood identity, and I carried it with me into adulthood.

What I didn't realize until years later was that my hunger for achievement was fueled by painful feelings of inadequacy. My need to achieve was propelled by a desire to overcome feelings of self-doubt, a deep sense of not being good enough. I was so afraid that others would discover my faults and shortcomings that I worked overtime to mask them. My hope was that being a superachiever would earn me the praise, recognition and acceptance I craved. Unconsciously, I was trying to win from others the love and respect that I didn't have for myself.

We all have intense longings. We long to be safe, to be protected from harm, to be shielded from life's unpredictability. We want to belong, to be freed from our fear of abandonment, to be part of a caring circle of friends. We ache to be loved just as we are, cherished for our uniqueness, treasured as the very one we are. We want to make a difference, to contribute something worthwhile, to leave something valuable as a legacy. We thirst for meaning and purpose, for some understanding of the why of life, for a way to make sense of our experience. We ache to encounter God and to develop a deep and personal relationship with our Creator and Redeemer.

As we attempt to personalize this Gospel, we are confronted by deep and unfulfilled longings, hungers that are difficult to name. When we are in the grip of these longings, it is easy to lose perspective and look for fulfillment in all the wrong places. As we connect with Jesus' experience of desert hunger and temptation, we begin to own up to the power of our longings and the way they shape our lives. As we join him in centering our longings on God, we begin to regain our bearings. His example reminds us that our true identity can only be found in God. Centuries ago Saint Augustine said it well: "You have made us for yourself, and our heart is restless until it rests in you."[3] What Jesus' first temptation makes clear is that God, and only God, is the authentic fulfillment of our longing.

WHERE WILL YOU PLACE YOUR ULTIMATE TRUST?

In facing the second temptation, Jesus refuses to put God to the test by asking for a diving catch. He embraces the vulnerability of his humanness and places a deep trust in God. It is hard to have enough confidence in one we love not to demand a sign. Our fears and insecurities can easily lead us to resort to control and manipulation.

The movie *The Birdcage*[4] portrays a manipulative love relationship between two gay men. Albert, played by Nathan Lane, is the star performer in the club that he and his partner Armand own. Armand, played by Robin Williams, directs the performances in which Albert stars. As the story unfolds, we see a very insecure Albert attempt one manipulation after another to trap Armand into elaborate displays of affection. No matter what Armand does, it isn't enough. Albert always wants more.

This comedy makes us laugh at such an extreme portrayal of insecurity. It also holds up a mirror to our relationships. We've all been involved in manipulative relationships—sometimes manipulating and at other times being manipulated. The weaker our confidence—in ourselves and in the other—the more likely we are to resort to such tactics. In facing the second temptation Jesus models a depth of confidence in God that refuses such manipulation. By contrast, Albert exemplifies a level of insecurity that can't avoid trying to control Armand to get what he wants.

The way that we pray is a powerful indicator of whether our relationship with God is characterized by manipulation or trust. When prayer is characterized by manipulation, it is self-centered, focuses on what I want and tries to bargain with God. When prayer is characterized by trust, it is centered on God, focuses on opening ourselves and letting go, and leads to surrendering to God's will.

We all face moments—just as Jesus did in the desert—in which we are tempted to avoid the painful realities of being human. In these moments our prayer can easily digress into bargaining with God. We want to control the uncontrollable—both life and God. So we try to cut a deal. When Jesus faces this temptation, he refuses to put God to the test by engaging in manipulative tactics. He does not become a jealous, insecure lover who needs continuous demonstrations of affection. Rather, he models a powerful faith that trusts deeply in God and surrenders to the divine will.

As we attempt to personalize this Gospel, we are confronted with a choice. Will our insecurities lead us to bargain with God for diving catches or other reassurances? Or, will we place our trust in God and surrender?

WHAT KINGDOM WILL YOU SERVE?

In personalizing the story of Jesus' third temptation, we face the same question that he did: What kingdom will we serve? Will we give ourselves—heart and soul—to the kingdoms of this world and strive for wealth and dominating power? Or will we devote ourselves to serving the kingdom of God and use our power to liberate and serve?

One summer while I was in college, I worked on a ministry team that served a group of churches in West Michigan. One evening, a family from one of the churches invited all five members of our team to dinner. It was a great evening of hospitality. Their surroundings made it clear that the family members were poor, but their hearts were rich in generosity. We shared a simple meal, played with the children, toured the small farm where they struggled to make ends meet and enjoyed good conversation.

Late that evening, as we returned to the house after watching the sunset, homemade bread was just coming out of the oven. The smell was wonderful, and the taste was even better. The five of us quickly devoured our first slice, and our hostess offered us another. I had just taken a bite out of my third slice when I overheard the youngest child say to her brother, "I hope there's enough left for breakfast." I almost choked on the bread.

For me that evening was a powerful experience of the difference between rich and poor. This poor family freely opened their hearts to us and shared generously what little they had. They were delighted to have us as their guests. As members of the ministry team we didn't consider ourselves rich, but in comparison to this family we certainly were. It had never occurred to any of us that this family would share food with us until it was gone. We might have been the ministry team, but on that evening they were the teachers. They gave us far more than dinner and homemade bread. They taught us a lesson about the deeper meaning of hospitality and why the poor find favor in God's eyes.

What's at stake here is whether or not we can personalize Jesus' third temptation by rejecting wealth and embracing the kingdom of God. For those of us who worry more about our investment portfolios than about whether we have daily bread, this temptation is even more seductive. Our wealth tempts us to serve the kingdoms of this world and our own egos. When we face that temptation, we have to be able to let go of wealth for the sake of the kingdom of God. The more attached we are to our lifestyle and possessions, the harder this letting go becomes.

HOW DOES THIS STORY CALL ME TO LIVE?

As you try to make the story of Jesus' temptation in the desert a part of your life, here are some questions to live and a Prayer from the Wilderness.

Living the Questions

One or more of the following questions may help you more fully personalize the story of Jesus' temptation in the desert.

- What wildernesses have I experienced in my life—times when my fears loomed large, my humanness was fully exposed and I felt at risk?

- When I experience "wilderness moments" in prayer and I don't know what to do, how do I respond? Am I able to embrace the silence and surrender to God?

- What temptations distract me from focusing my longing on God? Am I tempted by food, possessions, the desire for acceptance, sexual desire, power, wealth or something else?

- In what ways am I tempted to avoid the painful realities of being human and ask God for diving catches?

- What kingdom is my heart and soul set on serving?

- To what extent am I using my personal power to pursue selfish interests and build up an earthly kingdom? To what extent am I using that power to liberate and serve others?

Entering Into Prayer

Reflecting on the story of Jesus' temptation led me to this prayer:

PRAYING THE PRAYER FROM THE WILDERNESS

Spirit of God, you led Jesus into the wilderness and were with him in temptation. Be with me in the wilderness of my own life. Give me the courage I need to seek out prayer and solitude, even when I would prefer superficial distractions that keep me safe. Let me be strong in the face of temptation, help me focus my energy and attention on you, and keep me faithful to you and true to myself.

Jesus, you are God's compassionate presence. You know my deepest longings, what I ache for in my heart of hearts. You know how intense these longings are; help me focus them on you. I am so easily swayed by temptation, chasing after things that fail to satisfy. Help me recognize that my deepest hunger isn't about food, won't be satisfied by achievement or recognition and doesn't require the approval of others. Keep me true to my deepest longings and help me focus them on you alone. Give me the wisdom to know, as Augustine knew, that "you have made us for yourself, and our heart is restless until it rests in you."[3]

Jesus, you model fidelity in the face of temptation. There must be times when I really try your patience. When I am anxious and afraid, I want reassurances from you to prove that I can trust you. My will is strong. I want what I want, and I will resort to manipulation and bargaining in order to get it. I put you to the test in all kinds of crazy ways. Yet, you stay faithful to me through it all, loving me unconditionally. Give me the courage to trust your love.

Jesus, you know how seductive power and wealth can be. In the midst of temptation you had the strength to opt for freeing captives and serving the poor. Strengthen my resolve when wealth, power and the desire to build up my own earthly kingdom tempt me. Help me set my heart on the kingdom of God. Your kingdom come, your will be done.

Jesus, keep me poor in spirit so that I may see everything as your gift and offer it back to you in return. Give me a grateful heart that finds joy in every breath I take. Keep me from chasing after false gods and building earthly kingdoms. Free me from my preoccupation with wealth and possessions. Let me live a simple life as your disciple, a life that gives you praise and thanks.

Wonderful Creator, you have gifted me with many talents. So often I see those talents as "mine" and use them for my own purposes. Help me recognize that you have given me these gifts for a deeper purpose. Let me focus them on your will and your kingdom. Give me the courage to use them to liberate those held captive and to serve those in need.

CHAPTER TWO

GLIMPSES OF GOD TOUCHING US

The Transfiguration of Jesus (Matthew 17:1–9)

WHAT'S THE EXPERIENCE OF THE STORY?

Setting the Scene

The Transfiguration occurs at a transitional point in Jesus' ministry. The transition began six days before when Peter proclaimed Jesus to be the Christ at Caesarea Philippi. The disciples have begun to grasp that Jesus is the Messiah, but they are still struggling to understand the full meaning of that identity. Jesus is now beginning to reveal a new dimension of what being the Messiah means—one that the disciples find hard to swallow. He must suffer and die.

The Transfiguration story portrays Jesus as a "mountain man." Religious leaders in the Jewish tradition "go to the mountain." The mountain is the place where they encounter God in a direct and personal way. Moses encountered God on Mount Sinai, and he signifies the era of Hebrew history characterized by the law. Elijah experienced God both in a fiery sacrifice on Mount Carmel and in a whispering voice on Mount Horeb. He represents the prophetic era. Matthew's account of the Transfiguration portrays Jesus as an extension of this mountain tradition.

At the heart of this story is the revelation of Jesus as "my Son, the Beloved" (v. 5). It is the second of three such revelations that are defining moments in Matthew's Gospel. The first occurs at Jesus' baptism (Matthew 3:17) when the words are spoken by a voice from a cloud, and Jesus may be the only one who hears them. At the Transfiguration three of Jesus' closest disciples also hear the voice from the cloud saying the same words. The third revelation of Jesus as Son of God occurs at the moment of Jesus' death. The Roman centurion and the other soldiers presiding over his execution proclaim their faith that "truly this man was God's Son!" (Matthew 27:54).

Reading the Gospel

Read Matthew's account of Jesus' Transfiguration: Matthew 17:1–9.

Retelling the Story

The Transfiguration story opens with Jesus taking Peter, James and John "up a high mountain" (v. 1). They go off "by themselves" (v. 1), leaving the other disciples and the crowds behind. Jesus chooses these three to experience the Transfiguration, and the other disciples only hear about it after it has occurred.

For those of us who don't immediately grasp the mountain imagery, Matthew's narrative seems abrupt. Without warning, "Jesus is transfigured before them" (v. 2). There is a brilliant light. Jesus' "face shone like the sun," and his "clothes became dazzling white" (v. 2). Matthew is trying to describe a light more intense than anything experienced on earth. "Suddenly" (v. 3) Moses and Elijah appear. Matthew uses the word "suddenly" twice in just two verses (vv. 3, 5). The divine vision ambushes the disciples, catching them off guard. They are completely unprepared for this amazing experience. Such revelations of God are a pure gift. There is nothing we can do to earn or deserve such a wonderful, ecstatic experience.

Jesus engages Moses and Elijah in conversation, but Matthew gives us no clue as to what they talked about. This portrayal of Moses, Elijah and Jesus talking together conveys the sense that they have an intimate relationship. It demonstrates the continuity of God's revelation—from the Law of Moses through the prophetic tradition that Elijah represents to God's revelation in Jesus. This event dramatizes that the age of the Messiah has begun. Jesus' teaching announces it, and his healing ministry helps bring it about.

Ultimately, it will reach its fullness in Jesus' suffering, death and resurrection.

Peter is captivated by the vision. With characteristic enthusiasm he exclaims: "[I]t is good for us to be here" (v. 4). Then he asks Jesus if he should build three dwellings or tents—one for Moses, one for Elijah and one for Jesus. It's easy to identify with Peter's desire to make this moment last. The feeling of ecstasy is so wonderful that Peter wants to linger here and cling to it. Like Moses in the presence of the burning bush, Peter recognizes that he is on holy ground, a place where God is profoundly present.

Before Peter even finishes speaking, "suddenly a bright cloud overshadowed them" (v. 5). The vision unfolds quickly, and a voice from the cloud reveals Jesus' identity. "This is my Son, the Beloved; with him I am well pleased" (v. 5). The vision is a strong parallel to Jesus' baptism, yet this time it is witnessed by the three disciples. In addition to conveying Jesus' identity as the beloved Son, this powerful revelation indicates God's delight with him.

In the Transfiguration revelation the voice adds a phrase that isn't included in the baptismal account: "Listen to him" (v. 5). The voice from the cloud speaks these words directly to the three disciples—and through them to us. The experience is too much for them, and they fall to the ground overcome by fear. The story depicts the revelation of God as both fascinating and terrible. Moments before, Peter wanted to linger here and cling to the experience. Now he and the others fear for their lives.

As Peter, James and John cower in fear, Jesus touches them and provides reassurance: "Get up and do not be afraid" (v. 7). The vision is fleeting. They have received a remarkable gift, but it has passed. It may change their lives, but they will never experience anything quite like it again in this life. They are alone with Jesus, tangled up in a jumble of such emotions as fear, amazement, excitement, bewilderment and confusion.

As they gather themselves and start down the mountain, Jesus gives them a tall order: "Tell no one about the vision until after the Son of Man has been raised from the dead" (v. 9). How can they possibly keep this to themselves? They have just experienced God in a more powerful way than any of them had imagined was possible, and now Jesus is forbidding them to speak of it.

As they continue down the mountain, the disciples try to sort out what happened and determine what it means. Jesus helps them make sense of things. He also brings up the reality of his suffering and death. It is the lot of the prophet to suffer, and Jesus is no exception. He will suffer and die at the hands of those who fail to grasp his identity and mission. The disciples have been to the mountain and experienced Jesus in an amazing moment of glory. The power of that vision will need to strengthen their faith so that they can endure the suffering, doubt, confusion and death that will follow all too soon.

HOW DOES THE STORY TOUCH ME?

As I reflect on how the story of Jesus' Transfiguration touches my life, here are some of the ways that I connect with the experience of the story.

A Glimpse of Divine Majesty

For Peter, James and John the Transfiguration is a glimpse of divine majesty. Connecting with the experience of the story calls us to explore our own experiences of the rich and varied ways that God touches our lives.

As you look over your life, are there any events or series of events that you would describe as God touching you?[1] Perhaps you didn't recognize God's presence at the time, but as you look back now with the benefit of hindsight, what are those experiences?

When I reflect on this question, I can identify any number of God-touching-me experiences. When I was a sophomore in college, our associate pastor invited me to teach a religious education class for high school freshmen. I thought he was crazy to ask, and I'm not sure my first students benefited from their rookie teacher. What surprised me, though, was how that invitation changed my life. It launched me on a spiritual journey that continues to give meaning and direction to my life. Now that nearly forty years have passed since that invitation, I realize that the priest wasn't as crazy as I thought. There was no blinding vision, but I know now that it was definitely God touching me.

I had another God-touching-me experience in my early twenties. Four of us were returning home after visiting friends in another city. It was well after midnight, and I was driving. Everyone else in the car was asleep. My head began to nod, but I didn't have the good sense to ask someone else to take the wheel. The next thing I remember is hearing a passenger in the backseat yell my name. He jerked me back to attention just in time to negotiate an S-curve at sixty miles per hour. In another few seconds our lives and those of our families would have been changed forever. Some might name that a close call or a lucky break. I named it "God touching me."

Our goal in living the spiritual life is to learn to recognize God touching us in the everyday experiences of our lives. That touch doesn't have to be as dramatic or life-changing as the two I've just recounted. My list of "God touches" is a long one. In addition to a few dramatic experiences, it includes many simple yet profound moments such as prayerful sunrises, strangers who took the risk to smile, unexpected gifts and surprise encounters. These God-touching-me experiences range from subtle to dramatic, and they cover my entire life.

Although blinding visions that give us a glimpse of the divine majesty are wonderful, they are not the essence of the spiritual life. Our attempt to live a spiritual life begins with striving to recognize

God's presence in the everyday fabric of our lives. This ability to see with the eyes of faith has more to do with the ordinary than the spectacular.

Think back over your life...over today...over the last hour.... What are the experiences that you would describe as God touching you? As you let that question guide your exploration of God's presence in your life, it will help you recognize the many ways that God is with you every day. Cultivating the eyes of faith and attempting to see God in the everyday is a core discipline of the spiritual life. It is also the best way we have of preparing ourselves for our ultimate encounter with God in divine majesty.

My Son, the Beloved

The Transfiguration reveals that Jesus is God's beloved Son and that God is delighted with him. As I try to connect with this aspect of the story, I am aware of how deeply I long for the same affirmation—to be God's beloved and to find favor in God's eyes. In spite of this longing, I am also confronted by a painful inner conflict. My longing to be loved is met with a nagging fear that I don't measure up. When I am in the shadow of this fear, I find myself feeling deeply flawed and believe that there is something wrong with me.

The late actor Anthony Quinn recounts his struggle with this type of inner conflict in his moving self-portrait, *The Original Sin*.[2] At the height of his success as an actor—even though he has won two Academy Awards—he is deeply conflicted and struggles with love. "To give love and to accept love unconditionally—that to me is the highest goal. To be unable to love unconditionally—that to me is the original sin, the one that engenders all others," he says.[3]

His inner struggle is so intense that he is haunted by an imaginary ten-year-old boy who appears to him and taunts him. Nothing Quinn does is good enough to satisfy the kid. Whenever Quinn tries to accept love, the boy appears to tell him he is unworthy of it. Whenever he tries to claim happiness, his inner assassin recites a litany of reasons why he doesn't deserve it.

Like Quinn, I also have an inner assassin—a nagging inner voice that refuses to leave me alone. My self-doubt and self-hate reveal themselves in this voice as they belittle my achievements and sabotage my happiness. You may have an inner assassin too—that persistent voice of inner doubt that tries to cripple you with poisonous self-talk whenever you start to feel good about yourself.

God embraces our inner assassin with a startling message: "I love you just as you are—with no strings attached, without condition or limit." We are, as Henri Nouwen puts it, the beloved of God.[4] "My only desire is to make these words reverberate in every corner of your being—'You are the Beloved.'"[5] Sometimes the inner assassin is shouting so loudly that it drowns out this voice of God's embracing love. How can we possibly trust that God loves us just as we are? This revelation seems too good to be true. Our gut instinct is that there has to be a catch, that we can't possibly be God's beloved. Personalizing this story calls us to trust God's unconditional love enough to open ourselves and receive it with outstretched arms.

My experience as a grandfather has helped me grasp something of God's unconditional love for us. The way that I delight in my grandchildren has helped me connect with God's delight in us. It has helped me trust God's voice and cope with my inner assassin.

I love playing with my grandchildren—reading stories with them, taking them on outings and spending time with them in whatever way they want to spend it. My delight often takes the form of wonder when I see them do something that expresses their uniqueness. I find myself watching them and saying to myself: "Wow! That is so cool!" I don't understand this amazing bond with my grandchildren, and I certainly can't explain it. I just know that they have an uncanny knack for melting my heart.

My love for my grandchildren is remarkably unconditional—just like God's love for each of us. There is nothing they have done to earn or deserve my love. They had it before they were born, and it continues to grow with each experience we share. That love just is, and there is nothing that can take it away. If I can feel such deep love for these special ones in my life, how much more is God capable of having those feelings for us? Being a grand-father helps me trust that there are things that I do that cause God to exclaim, "Wow! That is so cool!"

Ultimately, each one of us is called to trust the subtle voice of God's love rather than the demeaning messages of the inner assassin. God's voice tells us that we are the beloved, surrounded by unconditional love. Yet if we long to find favor in God's eyes, something more is required of us. We are called to discern our unique mission in life. This discernment requires that we enter into a prayerful relationship with God to discover the highest and best use of our gifts. Discernment is a difficult and painstaking process. Sometimes we will get it right, and other times we will find ourselves on the wrong path. Our willingness to embrace the challenge of discernment causes God to exclaim, "Wow! That is so cool."

Listen to Jesus

Three words are at the heart of the transfiguration revelation: "Listen to him" (v. 5). My experience of these three words can be summed up in four: *Easier said than done.*

The Hebrew audience of Matthew's Gospel was deeply familiar with the rich theme of "listen to him" and would have immediately resonated with it. This notion conveys the imperative of giving God one's full attention, of wholeheartedly surrendering to God's will. This attentive listening is at the heart of God's covenant with the people of Israel. Because the people of Israel are God's people, they bend their ears to God's word and live out that word—both individually and as a people.

A friend of mine has a clever line he uses when he can't wait to express his point of view: "Don't talk while I'm interrupting." People usually laugh, and that pause allows him to jump in and claim the floor. Ironically, I have found that his comment is also a remarkably accurate description of my prayer. All too often my prayer consists of bombarding God with words. In effect, I'm saying to God, "Don't talk while I'm interrupting." My verbal barrage makes it hard for God to get a word in edgewise. If I take the voice from the cloud seriously, I need to learn to listen in prayer. My prayer has to become less verbal, less focused on what I want and more open to the way God speaks to me.

I struggle with prayer as listening. My life is busy, and my agenda is usually full. This results in several tendencies that inhibit listening prayer. The first is simply the difficulty of slowing down. When I am a whirlwind of activity plowing through my list of things to do, my prayer usually digresses into a series of requests for help. Help me find the courage to face this situation...Help me make the right decision...Help me learn to...There's nothing wrong with the prayers I utter quickly while walking down the hall to see a client or driving to my next appointment, but they don't leave much room for listening.

My second problem with listening prayer is distraction. When I try to quiet myself and listen, it doesn't necessarily go well. It's one thing to get my body to sit still. My mind—well, it has a mind of its own. While my body is in the chair, my mind continues to race around in all directions. My attempt at listening prayer often goes something like this: "Wonderful God, quiet me...oops, I forgot to call a client...Help me focus my attention on you...that report is due tomorrow morning, and it's not even close to being ready...

Creator God, I turn to you...my granddaughter's birthday is next week, and I wonder if she'd like..."

My hunch is you've had enough similar experiences that you get the idea. Listening prayer is, as I've already said, easier said than done.

Counteracting these two problems with listening prayer are two secrets to make it a deeper part of our lives. The first is that we don't have to be good at listening prayer; we just have to keep doing it. McNeil, Morrison and Nouwen reinforce this learning by stressing that "discipline and discipleship can never be separated.... They strengthen and deepen each other."[6] A disciple is one with a discipline. Even when our attempts at prayer are feeble and inadequate, it is important for us to stick with this discipline.

The second secret of listening prayer is that God finds a way to get through to us. The effectiveness of our prayer doesn't depend on our stumbling efforts. God is faithful and persistent. In spite of our weaknesses and difficulties, God gets through to us. Our attempts at listening prayer are the ways that we dispose ourselves to God's presence. God alone controls when and how those efforts bear fruit. Our trust needs to be in God, not in our own skill or even in our persistence.

Coming Down the Mountain

As the disciples start down the mountain after the Transfiguration, they are forced to come to grips with an experience that has overwhelmed them. Even though I have never had a dramatic, transfiguration-like experience of God, I understand something of what they must have experienced. I've had overwhelming experiences—the kinds that turn you upside down and leave you struggling to figure things out. Whether those experiences are wonderful or traumatic, they leave you confused and disoriented. They change you in ways you don't understand, and you are forced to make some sense of them.

One such overwhelming experience overtook me in early May of 1980. It was a beautiful spring day—the kind of day that those of us who live in snow country wait for all winter long. The beauty of the day lulled me into complacency, and I was totally unprepared when things turned ugly.

The tornado warning came shortly before 3:00 P.M. A warning means you take cover, but we get used to them. Usually, nothing happens. I had a meeting in another building of the office complex where I worked, so I decided to go to the basement in that building. As I left the building I was in, I realized that the day was totally still—not a breath of wind moving, not even the sound of a bird singing. I was surrounded by an eerie silence and overshadowed by a frightening sky. Instinctively, I found myself running to cover the short distance to the other building. As the people in that building headed for the basement, one of my coworkers had waited upstairs for me. Less than sixty seconds after the two of us got to the basement, we heard a freight train pass overhead—the signature sound of a tornado. After that, silence. It was gone as quickly as it had come.

As we rushed back upstairs, I was confronted by dramatic contrasts that were almost impossible to comprehend. The sky was blue and birds were singing again. Yet, the buildings in our complex looked like a bomb had hit them. The two buildings I had run between moments before were totally destroyed. Unbelievably, no one in our complex was injured. Others in the area weren't so fortunate. Five people died in that tornado. In its aftermath I was left to cope with the overwhelming sense that I had very nearly been its sixth victim.

In the days that followed, I had to grapple with the thoughts and feelings that accompany an overwhelming experience. I was unable to absorb my tornado experience all at once. As the disciples started down the mountain after the Transfiguration, they were faced with the same struggle. Their glimpse of divine majesty was an over-whelming experience that had taken them completely by surprise. Now they had to deal with their feelings and make some sense of what had happened.

On the way down the mountain, Jesus does several things to help the disciples through this fragile time. The first is quite surprising: He orders them to "tell no one about the vision until the Son of Man has been raised from the dead" (v. 9). It's hard to imagine the difficulty of not telling anyone. It wouldn't be too difficult to avoid telling the crowds, but not telling the other disciples would be excruciating. Imagine Peter—impetuous, lead-with-your-chin Peter—trying to obey Jesus' order. James and John might manage it, but Peter? Imagine how difficult it would be to deflect the curiosity of the other disciples when the three of them returned from the mountain with dazed looks and tight lips.

Jesus had his reasons for giving this command, but we can only guess at them. My hunch is that he knew that the three disciples needed that glimpse of divine majesty to stay steadfast in their belief during the suffering and death to come. Jesus may have been betting that if these three could make it through, the others would also have a chance. Yet to me there's more to Jesus' tell-no-one order than that. I think he realized that the Transfiguration had overwhelmed the three, and he didn't want their inability to handle the experience to mess things up. If they had come down the mountain with stars in their eyes and started talking nonsense, it would have made the other disciples jealous and confused the crowds. Better to give the three the time they needed to deal with this overwhelming experience. Better to give them the perspective they needed to understand it and some resurrection insight so that they could handle it appropriately.

The next thing Jesus did was engage Peter, James and John in a teaching dialogue to help them make sense out of what had occurred. The story gives us a short description of Jesus and the disciples debriefing their mountaintop experience. It helps us grasp what their dialogue might have been like. The disciples asked questions such as: "Why, then, do the scribes say that Elijah must come first?" (v. 10). In response, Jesus provided new insights into the events that were unfolding, and he helped them grasp the deeper meaning of those events: "but I tell you that Elijah has already come, and they did not recognize him" (v. 12). This debriefing gave Jesus a wonderful teaching opportunity, and he used it to nurture the disciples' spiritual growth and prepare them for ministry.

Finally, Jesus concluded the debriefing on a chilling note: "…the Son of Man is about to suffer…" (v. 12). If the three disciples still had any hope of remaining on the mountaintop, Jesus extinguished it. He may have been the beloved Son, but that identity did not let him escape the realities of being human or avoid the prophet's fate. The example of John the Baptist was all too clear in the memory of Peter, James and John. Jesus' sobering words made clear that he would also suffer at the hands of the authorities. It's hard to imagine anything that would have brought the disciples back down to earth more quickly than this warning.

Some years ago I heard Father Mike Kolar give a presentation to conclude a large youth convention. Several thousand young people were present, and they were on fire with energy and enthusiasm. For them the conference had been a mountaintop experience. Father Mike understood that his role was to help them down the mountain. He crafted his presentation carefully, and its title conveyed its core message: "Before You Rush Out to Save the World, Don't Forget to Clean Your Room."[7]

As we attempt to devote ourselves to the spiritual life, a few of us may be gifted with a mountaintop experience, an unearned glimpse of the divine majesty. The true challenge of the spiritual life, however, is not found in going to the mountain. It's found in devoting consistent time and energy to listening to God and learning to recognize the many ways that God touches us every day. That challenge does not lead us to seek out mountaintop experiences. It calls us begin our efforts to save the world by cleaning our own rooms.

HOW DOES THIS STORY CALL ME TO LIVE?

As you try to make the story of Jesus' Transfiguration a part of your life, here are some questions to live and a suggestion for entering into listening prayer.

Living the Questions

One or more of the following questions may help you live the story of Jesus' Transfiguration more fully.

• As I reflect on the story of Jesus' Transfiguration, what experiences in my own life come to mind? How do these experiences deepen my understanding of the transfiguration story?

• As I look back over my life, are there any events or series of events that I would describe as God touching me? Even if I didn't recognize God's presence at the time, as I look back now with the benefit of hindsight, where do I see God touching me?

• Have I ever experienced "the inner assassin," the poisonous self-talk that tries to cripple me? If so, what was that experience like? How do I cope with my inner assassin?

• What is my experience with listening prayer? In what ways do I find it helpful? In what ways is it difficult for me? What steps could I take to deepen my resolve to listen to Jesus?

• Have I ever experienced something—such as a tornado, falling in love or the birth of a child—that totally overwhelmed me? In what way was my experience of being overwhelmed like the Transfiguration experience of Peter, James and John?

• As the disciples came down the mountain, they had to sort things out and make sense of what had happened. Have I ever had a similar experience? If so, how did I respond to it? What did I do to gain understanding and perspective?

Entering Into Prayer

Here's a suggestion for using the Transfiguration story to enter into prayer:

PRAYING THE LISTENING PRAYER

Find a quiet, comfortable place where you can take some time by yourself. Think about the space that will be best for you. During the winter my favorite place is the den. In the summer I go outside on the deck. There are lots of options—Ignatius of Loyola often prayed while lying down.

Begin your prayer time by closing your eyes and breathing slowly and deeply. Pay attention to the rhythm of your breathing. Feel the air flowing into your lungs and back out again. Try to focus on these simple rhythms to become quiet and block out distractions.

Slowly repeat a few simple words to yourself. As you inhale, pray the words: "Help me trust you." As you exhale, pray the words: "I surrender." When you find yourself distracted, be patient. Gently bring yourself back to your breathing and to these simple words.

As you become calm and focused, you may want to become less verbal. Simply pray the word "trust" as you inhale and the word "surrender" as you exhale.

As your prayer deepens, you may choose to let go of the words altogether. Try to empty yourself, giving God your full attention. Relax, and trust the prayer. Wait for God to speak to you. I find that when I try too hard, I am focusing on my own efforts rather than giving God room to work.

See where this listening prayer leads you. Sometimes I find that it brings me new insight and direction. Other times it quiets me so that I am ready to read a Scripture passage with more openness. Sometimes I follow my listening prayer by writing in my journal. The beauty of listening prayer is that it creates a readiness to pray in a variety of ways.

I often limit my listening prayer to a certain length of time. You might want to start with ten minutes. I rarely spend more than twenty minutes in the listening prayer before going on to reading Scripture, writing in my journal or having a heart-to-heart conversation with God.

I have a word of caution. Don't place too much weight on what happens in your first attempt to enter into listening prayer or in a single session of prayer. Remember, it is a discipline, not a miraculous event. Try it for a week, and then reflect on the ways in which it has been helpful. Modify your approach if necessary, then try it for another week. Trust that your commitment to it will somehow give God the opportunity to speak to you.

CHAPTER THREE

ACKNOWLEDGING OUR DEEPER THIRST

Jesus Meets the Woman at the Well (John 4:5–42)

WHAT'S THE EXPERIENCE OF THE STORY?

Setting the Scene

The success of Jesus' ministry is growing, and he's starting to attract the attention of the authorities. He knows attention will lead to trouble, and it's too soon for that. So he and his disciples leave Judea for Galilee. In this more remote region he hopes to find the freedom he needs to pursue his ministry. The shortest route to Galilee takes them through Samaria.

The climate is hot and dry, and water is scarce. Jacob's well is at a crossroads near a Samaritan village. A well is a precious resource, essential for sustaining life. The people of the village walk a few minutes to the well each day to get the water they need. Travelers depend on the well to refresh themselves and provide water for their journeys.

On this particular day the well is the scene where an itinerant preacher named Jesus encounters a woman from the Samaritan village. She is going about her daily chores, trying her best to ignore a thirst that has shaped her life. He is on a mission, and his journey has left him tired and thirsty. Their meeting fills the story with the tension of a man ignoring cultural taboos to address a woman, a Jew disregarding issues of race and religious purity to interact with a Samaritan, and a teacher and healer reaching out to a woman with a questionable past. In the midst of this tension, their thirsts bring them together—at a deep well, where two roads meet, in a land where relationships are strained.

Reading the Gospel

Read John's account of Jesus meeting the woman at the well: John 4:5–42.

Retelling the Story

The story begins simply enough. The woman is fetching water as part of her daily routine. It is only as the story unfolds that we learn that she has a deeper thirst: She is desperate for a love that will last. This deeper thirst has shaped her entire life. Time and again, it has led her into relationships with men. Time and again, her hope for fulfillment has become a dead-end street. Each relationship has ended badly, and neither Jacob's well nor her bucket will satisfy this deeper thirst.

The woman's encounter with Jesus begins with his disarming request: "Give me a drink" (v. 7). This initiative is surprising—even shocking. The woman is taken aback by Jesus' directness, and her response challenges him. Perhaps she is trying to keep her distance. "How is it that you, a Jew, ask a drink of me, a woman of Samaria?" (v. 9). John adds a brief commentary to make sure that we don't miss the point: "(Jews do not share things in common with Samaritans)" (v. 9).

Jesus' response to the woman takes the encounter in a new direction: "If you knew the gift of God, and who it is that is saying to you, 'Give me a drink,' you would have asked him, and he would have given you living water" (v. 10). Always the teacher, Jesus builds on the experience of thirst and the image of water to reveal something of God's presence and his own identity. He urges the woman to grasp that there is more at stake in this encounter than drawing a daily ration of water from the well.

The woman doesn't understand Jesus' comment about living water. She attempts to interpret it literally—not realizing it's an image that reveals a deeper truth. Once again she challenges him:

"Sir, you have no bucket, and the well is deep. Where do you get that living water?" (v. 11). Jesus is talking about more than water from the well. He is talking about the gift of God that the woman so desperately needs: healing, forgiveness and unconditional love. This is the only gift that will quench her deeper thirst, a thirst that she can't yet imagine Jesus knows anything about.

The woman questions Jesus' identity. "Are you greater than our ancestor Jacob who gave us this well, and with his sons and his flocks drank from it?" (v. 12). If she were using the language of our time, she might have phrased her question like this: "Just who do you think you are?" At this point in the story, she sees herself as talking with a nameless stranger. Her comment may well be a put-down to keep this intruder in his place, but Jesus is not easily deterred. He returns to the woman's thirst and to his image of water, contrasting the water that he gives with the water the woman draws from the well. "Everyone who drinks of this water will be thirsty again, but those who drink of the water that I will give will never be thirsty. The water that I will give will become in them a spring of water gushing up to eternal life" (vv. 13–14). He is attempting to take the encounter to a new level. He knows she has a thirst that the water from this well has no power to quench, and he reaches out to her at the level of this deeper thirst.

The woman's next response reflects a change in her attitude. "Sir, give me this water, so that I may never be thirsty or have to keep coming here to draw water" (v. 15). For the first time, she is asking for something—shifting her stance from resistance to openness. Even though the woman has not yet grasped the true nature of this living water, she is intrigued. She is a long way from understanding what Jesus is talking about, but she has opened the door and admitted her thirst. The vulnerability of that admission gives Jesus the room he needs to work.

As soon as the woman opens herself by acknowledging her thirst and asking Jesus for living water, he makes a surprising request. "Go, call your husband, and come back" (v. 16). He is not changing the subject; he is going to the heart of her deeper thirst. The woman is desperate for a love that will last, and she has failed in every attempt to achieve it. This is the broken place in her life, the place where she is most vulnerable, the place where she is desperate for healing.

Even though the woman has begun to open herself up, she isn't ready to reveal the depth of her pain. She attempts to deflect Jesus' request that she call her husband by saying that she doesn't have a husband. Jesus responds to this deflection by affirming the truth of her statement. "You are right in saying, 'I have no husband'; for you have had five husbands, and the one you have now is not your husband" (vv. 17–18). The woman must have been dumbfounded: How can this stranger know so much about her? She acknowledges that this power of knowing must come from God: "Sir, I see that you are a prophet" (v. 19).

Next, the woman asks about a fundamental difference between the Jews and the Samaritans. "Our ancestors worshiped on this mountain, but you [Jews] say that the place where people must worship is in Jerusalem" (v. 20). She may be trying to change the subject in order to deflect attention from her painful past. More likely, her encounter with Jesus now takes on a broader purpose. Not only does she need the living water to quench her thirst for unconditional love, but her people must also drink the living water to quench their thirst for God. Her encounter with Jesus reveals that God's redeeming love extends beyond the Jewish people to all of Samaria and beyond.

As Jesus responds to her question, he makes clear that a new era is coming. In that era authentic worship will follow neither the

Jewish tradition nor that of the Samaritans. "Woman, believe me, the hour is coming when you will worship the Father neither on this mountain nor in Jerusalem" (v. 21). In the new era spirit and truth will characterize authentic worship, not a particular holy place or set of religious practices. "But the hour is coming, and is now here, when true worshipers will worship the Father in spirit and in truth, for the Father seeks such as these to worship him" (v. 23).

The woman is no stranger to the expectations that the Messiah's arrival will usher in a new era. "I know that Messiah is coming (who is called Christ). When he comes, he will proclaim all things to us" (vv. 25–26). She expects the Messiah, just as other Samaritans and the Jews do. Yet, she can hardly be prepared for Jesus' next statement: "I am he, the one who is speaking to you" (v. 26). Jesus asserts that he is the anointed one that Samaritans and Jews have been awaiting for generations.

The woman's experience of Jesus gives her the courage to trust him. Her greatest fear is that anyone who truly knows her will reject her. Yet Jesus knows everything about her—including her darkest secrets—and he embraces her with an unconditional love. She has an intense longing for a love that will last, but she has repeatedly been hurt by broken promises and failed relationships. Now she has met a man who loves her in a completely different way than she thought was possible. He may be the first man who has ever loved her without wanting to sleep with her.

The woman is accustomed to living in the shadows, avoiding painful confrontations and hedging the truth in order to protect herself. In Jesus she encounters a surprising directness that cuts through custom and convention to get to the truth. In her encounter with him she has come to know more about her own identity, how God is present and what her people's destiny is. The only way her experience makes sense is if she is in the presence of the Messiah. As unbelievable as Jesus' revelation may seem, she recognizes the truth in his words.

Overcome by this experience, the woman "left her water jar and went back to the city" (v. 28). She doesn't need the water jar anymore because she has received the living water. She has been redeemed, and her deeper thirst for a love that will last has been quenched. She returns to the city on a mission. The power of her experience is so overwhelming that she has to tell others about this stranger and how he has touched her life. "Come and see a man who told me everything I have ever done!" (v. 29).

The way she talks about Jesus is interesting. "He cannot be the Messiah, can he?" (v. 29). Perhaps it is too much to believe so quickly. More likely, she is using a question to arouse curiosity, inviting people to come and see Jesus. In effect, she's asking them to check him out and decide for themselves. What's remarkable is that, in spite of her past, the people of the village come to believe through her. She may have seemed the most unlikely person for Jesus to choose to reveal himself, but she has become an effective witness and evangelist.

HOW DOES THE STORY TOUCH ME?

As I reflect on the story of Jesus' encounter with the woman at the well, here are some of the ways that I connect with the experience of the story.

A Deeper Thirst

Like the Samaritan woman, we all have a deeper thirst for a love that will last. This search is so much a part of our lives that it pervades music, art, theater, television and movies. We turn on the radio and hear songs that express the thirst for love as well as those that grieve the pain of failed relationships. Whether love has left us fulfilled or frustrated, we know how precious it is.

The Samaritan woman's struggle to find a lasting love reminds me of a scene in the movie *The Big Chill*. Meg (played by Mary Kay Place) longs for love, but she has been unable to find a lasting relationship. In talking to her friend Sarah (played by Glenn Close), she sums up her frustration with relationships and her cynicism about men:

> ...They've just broken up with the most wonderful woman. Or, they've just broken up with a bitch who looks exactly like me. They're in a transition from a monogamous relationship, and they need space. Or, they're tired of space, but they just can't commit. Or, they want to commit, but they're afraid to get close. They want to get close, and you don't want to get near them.... I've been out there dating for twenty years. I've gotten where I can tell in the first fifteen seconds if there's a chance in the world.[1]

Like Meg and the Samaritan woman, I have a deeper thirst for a love that will last. Two broken places in my life fuel this deeper thirst: a childhood wound and a failed relationship.

We Are All Wounded

My attempt to connect with the story of the woman at the well, to personalize its meaning in my life, requires acknowledging that I am wounded.

For much of my childhood, my father struggled with an addiction to alcohol. His addiction and my family's struggle to cope with it were the unspoken focus of enormous amounts of our energy and attention. As a result of his struggle, I grew up with an unsatisfied thirst for my father's love. Sometimes he was physically absent, other times he was emotionally unavailable, and still other times his rage was fierce enough that I preferred his absence. I internalized his absence and his anger as a fear that I would be abandoned and as a belief that something was wrong with me. No matter what I did, it never seemed to be good enough.

As a result of these experiences, I carry within me the scars of a child who was deprived of his father's love. When I reflect on the story of the Samaritan woman, I connect with the pain of her wound. Like her, I know what it is like to live with shame, feel defective and want to find someplace to hide. She and I both know what it is like to need redemption. We both know how hard it is to trust a stranger, let ourselves be vulnerable and believe that we can be redeemed.

I also connect with the Samaritan woman because I know what it is to feel the pain of a failed relationship. In my mid-twenties I fell very much in love with a woman to whom I became engaged. In the weeks just before I finished graduate school, we faced a difficult decision: She had a teaching contract in California and my new job was in Michigan. We decided she would fulfill the contract and I would move. Our plan was that she would move to Michigan at the end of the school year, and we would marry the following summer.

Soon after I moved, I sensed that something just wasn't right. I had no idea what it was, but I could feel it. It was as though her second thoughts were listening in on our telephone conversations. During our time together over the Christmas holidays, she told me that she had decided to terminate our engagement.

I was devastated. Because of my childhood experience, I had not come to love easily. After being afraid of love for so long, I had finally taken the risk of letting myself fall in love. Now the relationship was ending against my will and in spite of my best efforts. I was forced to deal once again with the childhood feelings of anger, guilt, self-doubt and shame—the same feelings that the Samaritan woman must have faced. Deep inside I felt like there must be something wrong with me. I thought that, for some reason that I couldn't begin to grasp, love would never happen for me.

Like the woman at the well, we are all wounded. Our deeper thirst emerges from these broken places within us. The Samaritan woman had been wounded by a series of failed relationships. My wounds include the ache for my father's love and the pain of a broken engagement. You have your wounds too. The ways in which we have been wounded are deeply personal and unique. The experience of being wounded, however, is something we all have in common.

Choosing Our Response to the Wound

Because we are human, wounding is inevitable. The choice we face is not whether we will be wounded but how we will respond to our wounds. The choices we make shape our lives in powerful ways. The story of the woman at the well demonstrates three options we face: denying that we are wounded, getting stuck in our pain and opening ourselves to redemption.

Denial

One way we can respond to the experience of being wounded is to try to deny it. Early in the story, this is the approach that the Samaritan woman took. She tried to deny she had a husband in order to hide her wound. My childhood family taught me this approach: We denied that my father had a drinking problem, and we denied that his drinking hurt us.

It is easy to rationalize that denial is the best approach. Why would the woman get into all that messy stuff about husbands with a stranger? Why would my family subject itself to the kind of embarrassment that facing my father's drinking would entail? Denial is inviting, and it may even work—for a while. It isn't long, however, before the truths that have been hidden come back to haunt us. Like a high-interest loan, the required payments get bigger and bigger. As time passes, the energy required to maintain the denial increases; the cost of pretending not to see escalates.

My tendency to choose denial is very strong. It's hard for me to admit that I am wounded. Several years ago a coworker gave me a coffee mug for Christmas that depicts this tendency. The picture on it shows a cow lying on its back with its feet sticking straight up in the air. The caption under the picture says, "No, really, I'm fine." Like the cow on my mug and the woman at the well, my instinct for denial often overpowers my inclination to reveal my vulnerability. I understand why she tried to keep her conversation with the stranger superficial and go on about her business. Had I been at the well that morning, I might have succeeded in keeping the stranger from getting too close. By keeping my guard up, I would have cut myself off from the living water—missing Jesus' healing touch and redeeming power. There is a time to move beyond denial and opt for honesty and self-revelation. The woman recognized the moment, and we are called to do the same.

Getting Stuck

At the other end of the continuum from denying our wounds is another option: getting stuck in our pain. Even though pain is an inevitable consequence of being human, we don't have to wallow in it. Some people who experience pain are unable to move on, and they develop pain-based identities.

After my fiancée ended our engagement, I experienced getting stuck in my pain. I found myself angry and resentful, thinking that there was something wrong with me. Like the Samaritan woman, I was afraid that no one could know my deepest secrets and still love me. I told myself that if someone did love me, it would only be for a short time. Then, like my father and my fiancée, the person would abandon me.

For some dark and lonely years, I internalized this identity, clinging to my pain and refusing to risk another relationship. It took me a long time to realize that holding on to this pain-based identity was actually a way of attempting to continue a relationship that had ended. The pain was also a kind of protective cocoon that saved me from having to face the risk of another relationship.

Opening Ourselves to Redemption

Somewhere between denying our pain and getting stuck in it, we find a third option. We can open ourselves to redemption. This choice is the good news that the story of the Samaritan woman reveals. It is the choice that the story calls us to make.

As the story unfolds, we see that opening herself to redemption is not the woman's first instinct. We've already seen that her first instinct was to choose denial and try to avoid the stranger. It was the action of the stranger that gave her enough courage to risk making a different choice. The stranger's revelation that he knew everything about her meant she no longer had anything to hide. Her experience of the stranger's deep and unconditional love meant she no longer had any need to try to hide it. Finding herself in the safety of an unexplained intimacy, she acknowledged that she was wounded and gave the stranger the room to become a redeeming force in her life.

I struggle with this kind of vulnerability and self-revelation. My fear of abandonment causes me to resist being open and candid about who I am. I am still afraid of rejection. As a result, my tendency is to try to project an idealized image of myself—a cleaned up, no-zits version. When I have my choice of self-portraits, I select the idealized one in soft focus so that my flaws won't show. This struggle with admitting my vulnerability limits my ability to build intimate relationships—even with my family and friends. If I follow my instinct and resist letting them in on my struggle, I cut myself off from the love and support they can provide. I am like the Samaritan woman, unable to imagine that the stranger—or anyone else—could know all about me and not abandon me.

The word *intimacy* comes from the Latin phrase *in timore*. Its literal meaning is "into the fear." When we are on the verge of an intimate encounter, we are afraid. We face a choice: to enter into the encounter in spite of our fear or to run away. Every profound encounter—from a teenager's first date to Moses' encounter with the burning bush—brings us to the point of making this choice. The Samaritan woman faced this choice in responding to the stranger at the well. I face it in deciding whether to admit to my vulnerability or maintain my denial. All the profound mysteries of life—making friends, falling in love, facing death, experiencing God—involve this choice between safety and vulnerability. Embracing the way of redemption, which is the good news in this story, requires moving into this fear.

The Living Water of Redemptive Love

The core message of this story is that Jesus gifts us with the living water of God's redemptive love. This unique and powerful force— so different from anything the woman has named love before— heals, transforms and reconciles. The good news of the story is that this "love" which is the only thing that can satisfy the woman's deeper thirst—is revealed to her in the encounter with the Jesus, the living water.

Even though the woman has a desperate thirst for this love, she initially resists it. Through her encounter with a stranger, she is able to let go of her resistance and open herself to this remarkable gift. When she invites the stranger in, she surrenders to the transforming power of God's redemptive love. As we experience redemptive love, it calls us to change in four significant ways.

CHANGING OUR ORIENTATION TO LIFE

Through her encounter with the stranger, the woman's fundamental orientation toward life changes. At the beginning of the story, her pain and disappointment seem to have caused her energy to be focused inward. She has been burned, and she's become self-protective, even self-centered. Like most survivors, she has learned to take care of herself—but at a price. At the very least she is cautious; more likely, she is suspicious and expects to be disappointed. The woman's early responses to Jesus seem to indicate that she is defensive, even cynical.

The woman's fundamental orientation toward life changes as the story unfolds. She opens herself to receive the redemptive love that Jesus offers. She moves beyond defensiveness to acknowledge her deeper thirst and ask for living water. Her narrow, self-conscious concerns widen, and she explores the nature of authentic worship and the relationship between her people and the Jews. By the end of the story, this self-focused woman who had withdrawn from those around her is running back to the village to tell others how a stranger changed her life. Her orientation toward life is now fully outward. The outcast has become an evangelist; she has a new mission in life.

Like the Samaritan woman, our orientation toward life changes when we are touched by redemptive love. Earlier in this chapter I recounted my experiences of being wounded by both my father's abandonment and a failed relationship. Like the Samaritan woman, these experiences caused me to respond to others in self-protective ways, expecting to be disappointed. The change I've experienced in my own fundamental orientation toward life came slowly and gradually. I've never had a one-time encounter that led to the kind of dramatic transformation and healing that the Samaritan woman experienced at the well. For her, the living water was a waterfall. For me, it has been more like a long soak in a soothing bath. My gradual change has been nurtured by a number of strangers and friends over a period of years. But, my experience has also been powerful.

Over time, I have been able—at least on my good days—to let go of pain and move beyond the belief that there is something wrong with me. Over time, I have come to trust that I am deeply loved and reach out to others with renewed energy. The same redeeming power of God that touched the Samaritan woman has also touched me.

CHANGING OUR PATTERNS OF BEHAVIOR

The story portrays a dramatic change in the Samaritan woman's patterns of behavior. Like most of us, she tends to repeat her mistakes. She has lived through five failed marriages and is now in another relationship. With her track record, few of us would bet on her ability to change. Jesus takes the bet because he trusts the power of God's redemptive love. The turning point in the story comes when she trusts it too. This is the key change in her pattern of behavior. She moves from suspicion to trust. As a result, she opens herself to the stranger, receives the living water and surrenders to its transforming power. It is the woman's ability to trust, to receive and to surrender that creates the possibility of building a love relationship that will last.

The poet Edna St. Vincent Millay captures something of the Samaritan woman's experience with patterns of behaviors and the difficulty of changing them. "It is not true that life is one damn thing after another—it's one damn thing over and over."[2] I know how both of them feel. I find it's much easier to envision change and talk about it than it is to actually change. For years, I have kept a personal journal. A frequent theme in that journal is how—in both big and small ways—I'd like my life to be different than it is. Every major change in my life—from choosing marriage to making career decisions and exploring new hobbies—has found space in the pages of my journal long before finding room in my day-to-day life. As I look back through my journal after successfully making life changes, it's clear there was a long struggle to break my current habits and patterns in the process of establishing new ones. For many months during the change process, my life was one damn thing over and over. Finally, I either was so determined to change or so fed up with the status quo that I was able to let go of the security of the known and try something new.

CHANGING OUR CORE BELIEFS

In this story Jesus' redemptive love transforms the woman's core beliefs—about love, about herself and about God. Each of us has deeply ingrained beliefs that shape the way we see life and respond to it. Because the Samaritan woman has experienced numerous failed relationships, she has internalized certain core beliefs. The story doesn't reveal these core beliefs directly, but we can make some pretty good guesses about what they are.

On her way to the well, her beliefs about love may go something like this: Falling in love is wonderful, but it doesn't last. Men want to sleep with me, but soon I'll be abandoned and alone again. Whatever beliefs she brings to the well, we see strong evidence that these beliefs change as a result of her encounter with Jesus. In that encounter she experiences a different love than she has ever experienced before. As she is transformed, so are her beliefs about love. She may not have a language to describe what has happened, but she now knows a redemptive love that heals and transforms. For much of her life she has experienced something else she called love—a powerful force of attraction that was exciting but eventually left her alone and empty. Her encounter with Jesus changes her core beliefs about love.

The woman's encounter with Jesus also changes her core beliefs about herself. On her way to the well, she may well believe that something is wrong with her. Her past experience has taught her that as soon as a lover gets to know her, he abandons her. At the well she experiences a man who knows everything about her and loves her more deeply than she ever thought was possible. That encounter gives her an entirely different experience of herself, and it transforms her core beliefs about herself. She now knows that she is loved unconditionally for being the very one she is. Her past failures no longer matter. Her experience of being healed and transformed by redemptive love gives her the courage to believe in her own innate goodness. For the first time in her life, she is able to trust that she has found a love that will last.

Before her encounter with Jesus the woman may believe that God is distant and unconcerned about her pain. It's not that she doesn't believe in God; it's just that she's not sure whether God is present in her life and concerned about her. When she encounters Jesus, God touches her in a totally different way than she ever imagined. As a result, her fundamental beliefs about God change. By accepting Jesus as the Messiah, she is forced to come to grips with the reality that God is real and present, that God has visited her in the stranger at the well. God is no longer an abstract concept or a vague belief. Her encounter with Jesus reveals a God more present and loving than she had dared to believe was possible. One trip to the well dramatically changes her fundamental beliefs about God.

From my experience of growing up in a chemically dependent family, I know something of core beliefs and how they need to change. Through my struggles growing up, I developed the core belief that "I have the power to help myself." This core belief was quite helpful because it gave me the courage to cope with many difficult situations. Over time, however, it became less functional and took on a life of its own. As a young adult I had become so self-reliant that I couldn't accept help from others. By that time my core belief, which was deeply ingrained but only partially conscious, went something like this: "I have to do it all by myself...perfectly." This core belief demanded achievement, control, rugged individualism and perfection. It was a heavy burden loaded with guilt and stress that drove me to work too hard and expect too much of myself. When I acted on this core belief, my behavior often compromised my professional effectiveness and undercut my ability to build intimate relationships.

Slowly, as I became more conscious of this core belief, I came to grasp its negative impact on my life. I realized it left no room in my life for the gift another can give me or for the redemptive love of God. Over time, I have been able to modify this core belief somewhat. Now the statement that captures my core belief is: "I'll do what I can, with the help of God and others, and trust that good will come from my efforts." This new core belief embodies less control, more trust and more freedom. It also tries to leave more room for the redemptive love of God. I don't succeed in living out this core belief every day, but I'm learning and trying.

As we open ourselves to the redemptive love of God, we are called to examine our core beliefs and change the ones that fail to give God room to work. Like the woman at the well, we will find ourselves experiencing the unconditional acceptance of a God who loves us deeply. We will find ourselves letting go of control and learning to trust that God and others are there for us in surprising ways.

Receiving Emotional Healing

The woman comes to the well broken and hurting. Jesus embraces her with redemptive love, and she experiences a powerful healing. This healing isn't complete until it transforms her at an emotional level, at the level of her deepest feelings.

The most dramatic evidence we see of this emotional healing is the renewed energy and vitality that compel her to run back to the village and proclaim what has happened. This self-focused woman who avoided contact with the other villagers has moved beyond her preoccupation with safety to reach out to others and tell them what she has experienced. The living water has, indeed, become "a spring gushing up" within her (v. 14).

We don't know what touched the others in the village. Perhaps it was the passion in her voice as she told them about her experience at the well. Perhaps it was a joy that radiated from her as she spoke. All we know is that they believed her and went to see for themselves.

What seems clear is this: They would not have believed her if she had appeared to be broken, cynical and self-centered. The power of her testimony flowed out of the dramatic emotional healing that she experienced. As the people in the village sensed the transformation that had taken place in her, they wanted that transformation for themselves and sought out the source of it. If we are able to trust the healing power of God's redemptive love, we are touched at the emotional level. A whole new world of energy and emotion opens up to us. We find a deep, mission-focused energy welling up within us like a spring of living water.

How Does This Story Call Me to Live?

As you try to make the story of the Samaritan woman a part of your life, here are some questions to live and a prayer that invites you to surrender to God's redemptive love.

Living the Questions

One or more of the following questions may help you personalize the story of the woman at the well more deeply.

• What experiences in my life cause me to identify with the Samaritan woman?

• What is the deeper thirst that brings me to the well and reveals my true longing?

• How have my wounds opened me to the healing and redeeming touch of Jesus?

• What surprise encounters have I experienced that opened me to the healing and redeeming power of God?

• How have I been touched and changed by the power of God's redeeming love?

• In what ways have I experienced a transformation that resulted in renewed energy and passion—the kind of energy that led the Samaritan woman to run to the village and tell others what had happened?

Entering Into Prayer

JESUS, LIVING WATER

Jesus, Living Water, in my thirst I turn to you.

Jesus, Living Water, help me trust the surprising and unexpected ways that I encounter you. My thirst brings me to desert places where you are the stranger at the well. Yet my fear so easily closes me off from your redemptive love, and I find myself blocking your healing power. I often resist the very love I so desperately need. Give me the grace both to recognize that only your redemptive love will fulfill my deepest thirst and to open myself to that love. In my thirst I turn to you.

Jesus, Living Water, you know my deepest thirsts. You know all my secret places, even the corners where I hide in the darkness. There is nothing I can hide from you. You know how deeply I ache to belong, my longing for a love that will last and my need to be loved without condition or limit. In my thirst I turn to you.

Jesus, Living Water, thanks for those who love me with your redemptive love, especially those who to continue to love me even when I fail to return their love. Whether these are strangers or lifelong friends, I am grateful for the way they embody your redeeming love. Help me open myself to those who express your love, let go of my fear and resistance, and surrender to the transforming power of your love. In my thirst I turn to you.

Jesus, Living Water, help me move beyond my guilt and shame. Teach me to love myself with an unconditional love that heals, transforms and reconciles. For so much of my life, I have lived with the belief that there is something wrong with me. Help me open myself to your redeeming love, trust my own goodness and learn to love myself. In my thirst I turn to you.

Jesus, Living Water, give me the courage to live as one touched and changed by your redeeming love. Gift me with the passion and energy to run and tell others how your love has transformed me. Help me discover the mission that you call me to fulfill and let me embrace it with passion. In my thirst I turn to you.

Jesus, Living Water, in my thirst I turn to you.

CHAPTER FOUR
OPENING OURSELVES TO THE JESUS TOUCH
Jesus Heals the Man Born Blind (John 9:1–41)

WHAT'S THE EXPERIENCE OF THE STORY?

Setting the Scene

This story takes place in Jerusalem, most likely in the temple or near it. This is the center of the Jewish world, so it is no surprise that it becomes both a focal point for Jesus' ministry and the stage where the controversy between Jesus and the authorities unfolds. The conflict focuses on the signs that Jesus performs and the fact that he heals on the Sabbath. The story forces us to make a choice: Is Jesus' healing the work of God or a violation of the Sabbath?

A significant portion of this story is framed as a court proceeding. Witnesses are called, the man born blind's qualifications to testify are determined and facts are ascertained. Both the identity of the man and the fact that he was born blind are confirmed. The setting of a trial gives him the opportunity to testify to the healing that has taken place and to his belief that Jesus' works prove he is from God. The Pharisees preside over this "trial," and the story's irony is that their blindness prevents them from seeing the truth in the man's testimony.

The story makes clear that discipleship involves difficult choices. The man born blind is forced to choose between competing allegiances. He casts his lot with Jesus even though that means that he is thrown out of the synagogue and alienated from his parents. He models the disciple's call to testify to his faith in Jesus regardless of the cost. As we personalize this story, we are called to see in new ways and wrestle with the difficult choices.

Reading the Gospel

Read the story of the man born blind: John 9:1–41.

Retelling the Story

The opening words of this story are intriguing: "As he [Jesus] walked along..." (v. 1). Jesus doesn't appear to go out of his way to meet the man born blind. He encounters brokenness and need wherever he goes, and he responds with healing and mercy. When the disciples see the blind man, they raise a question about the cause of his physical infirmity. "Rabbi, who sinned, this man or his parents, that he was born blind?" (v. 2). The disciples' question is based on the prevailing view of the time—that physical impairment is a punishment for sin. They accept this view so completely that their only question is about whose sin it was.

Jesus' response goes deeper than their question. He contradicts the popular notion that physical infirmity is a punishment for sin— a view that is undoubtedly the belief and the teaching of the Pharisees. He provides a radically different explanation: "He was born blind so that God's works might be revealed in him" (v. 3). The man's infirmity provides Jesus with the opportunity to perform the work of God. He sees the man's blindness in the context of his mission of healing and reconciliation. Jesus' explanation opens the disciples to a new way of seeing blindness and other physical ailments. It also puts his teaching in sharp contrast to that of the Pharisees. From the second verse on, this story is about overcoming blindness and misconception to embrace new ways of seeing.

Jesus proceeds to heal the blind man. The description of his healing action is quite detailed. "[H]e spat on the ground and made mud with the saliva and spread the mud on the man's eyes" (v. 6). He then tells the man to "Go, wash in the pool of Siloam" (v. 7). The blind man trusts Jesus enough to follow his direction. When he washes in Siloam, his blindness is cured. This cleansing evokes images of baptism as well as healing. The man's sight is restored, and he is reborn as a disciple.

The cure sets off a series of controversies, and the man born blind finds himself in the midst of them. The first controversy involves whether a healing occurred and how it took place. When the man encounters his neighbors and those who have seen him begging, some believe he has been cured but others think he merely resembles the blind man. In attempting to settle this argument, he "kept saying, 'I am the man'" (v. 9). The people demand to know "how were your eyes opened?" (v. 10). The man provides the same detailed description of how Jesus performed the healing (v. 11) that was set forth earlier in the story (v. 6–7), but his description of the healing does little to settle things.

As the people bring the man to the Pharisees, a second controversy erupts: The healing took place on the Sabbath. The next part of the story is structured like a legal proceeding. The Pharisees preside over a trial-like inquiry to determine if the man has been healed and whether the Sabbath has been violated. During the proceeding, the Pharisees ask the man how he received his sight. Once again, he provides the same detailed explanation, (v. 15). The man's testimony leaves the Pharisees divided on a key question: whether or not Jesus is from God. Some of the Pharisees conclude that he cannot be from God because he doesn't observe the Sabbath. Yet others raise a difficult question: "How can a man who is a sinner perform such signs?" (v. 16). The Pharisees ask the man who has received his sight for his opinion of Jesus. "What do you say about him? It was your eyes he opened" (v. 17). The man is quick to testify to his belief about Jesus' identity: "He is a prophet" (v. 17).

The next twist in the story comes when the Jews call the man's parents as witnesses. "The Jews did not believe that he had been blind and had received his sight until they called the parents of the man" (v. 18). His parents' testimony is clear. "We know that this is our son, and that he was born blind" (v. 20). They do not comment on how he was healed or by whom. Instead, they direct the authorities to their son and confirm his qualifications as a witness. "Ask him; he is of age" (v. 21). The man's parents make clear that he possesses an essential characteristic of a disciple: "He will speak for himself" (v. 21).

The man born blind is called to testify a second time. The authorities demand that he "give glory to God!" (v. 24)—a formula used to confess guilt. For them his being born blind is evidence of his sinfulness. In addition, his testimony that Jesus is a prophet (v. 17) and therefore "from God" brings him under the sentence of expulsion from the synagogue. He is given an opportunity to recant. The Pharisees are now united in their assertion: "We know that this man (Jesus) is a sinner" (v. 24). The man born blind responds to their conclusion about Jesus by invoking his own experience of Jesus' healing touch: "I do not know whether he is a sinner. One thing I do know, that though I was blind, now I see" (v. 25).

A defining characteristic of being touched by Jesus is the ability to see. For the blind man, Jesus' touch resulted in physical healing, and he is now able to see. For other disciples, Jesus' touch transforms their view of the world, reveals the way God is present as a healing force and conveys spiritual insight. By contrast, the Pharisees are blind—unable to see the goodness of Jesus' works or recognize his origin in God.

When the authorities again begin to question the man about what Jesus did and how he received his sight, the man refuses to cooperate. "I have told you already, and you would not listen. Why do you want to hear it again?" (v. 27). No doubt the man's assertive response angered the authorities. His next statement brings the conflict to its climax: "Do you also want to become his disciples?" (v. 27). They revile the man and clearly state the division: "You are his disciple, but we are disciples of Moses" (v. 28).

The fundamental choice is now clear: Are you a disciple of Moses adhering to law and religious practice or are you a disciple of Jesus trusting he performs the works of God? The story offers no middle ground. The disciples of Moses "know that God has spoken to Moses, but as for this man [Jesus], we do not know where he comes from" (v. 29). The man born blind stands up strong to pose a different view:

> Here is an astonishing thing! You do not know where he comes from, and yet he opened my eyes. We know that God does not listen to sinners, but he does listen to one who worships him and obeys his will. Never since the world began has it been heard that anyone opened the eyes of a person born blind. If this man were not from God, he could do nothing. (v. 30–33)

The authorities dismiss the man's testimony by saying "You were born entirely in sins, and are you trying to teach us?" (v. 34). They are trapped in the misconception that the man's blindness is a punishment for sin. As a result, they renounce Jesus and drive the man out of the synagogue.

When Jesus hears that the man has been expelled from the synagogue, he seeks him out. During this second encounter, the man professes his faith in Jesus without hesitation and worships him.

As the story unfolds, it reveals both the gift of discipleship and its cost. The disciple receives Jesus' touch, is sent to bathe in healing waters and comes to see in new ways. Yet that healing comes at a price. As disciples we may find ourselves in the midst of trials and be required to witness to our faith in hostile settings.

HOW DOES THE STORY TOUCH ME?

As I reflect on the story of Jesus healing the man born blind, here are some of the ways that I connect with the experience of the story.

The Experience of Blindness

The story calls me to recognize the ways that I am blind. The type of blindness that I suffer from is not a physical infirmity—my eyes are healthy. The story, however, makes clear that there is more to seeing than having the physical attribute of sight. It helps us recognize our spiritual blindness.

In the classic story *The Little Prince,* the prince takes great care to tame the fox. Only then does the fox reveal his secret: "One sees clearly only with the heart. Anything essential is invisible to the eyes."[1] This biblical account is more than the story of a man whose physical blindness is healed. It is a story that invites us to see in a deeper way. Only if we can see with our hearts will we be able to perceive Jesus' healing touch and open ourselves to it. Our attempt to personalize this story begins with exploring spiritual blindness, the blindness that has more to do with the heart than with the eyes. We now explore two of the many ways that our hearts struggle to see rightly.

BLINDED BY OUR STANCE TOWARD LIFE

Some years ago I had the privilege of interviewing nursing home patients in an attempt to discover what gave them the ability to cope with the challenges of late age. During one of my conversations with a patient named Florence, I asked if she had a philosophy of life. She seemed somewhat put off by such a theoretical question, and she answered without hesitation: "No."

Trying a different approach, I drew on some of what I'd learned about Florence during my previous conversations with her.

"Florence, you've lived for almost ninety years. You've raised a family, suffered the loss of your husband, survived a stroke and experienced lots of other things that had to be very difficult. Through all these struggles, what gave you the courage to go on with life?"

This time Florence paused before she responded.

"I think that life is like me. I can look at the part of me that doesn't work [a reference to the side of her body paralyzed by stroke], and I can be angry. Or I can look at the side of me that does work, and I can be grateful."

Both Florence's response and the story of the man born blind reveal a deep truth about seeing. Our perception of reality is profoundly shaped by our stance toward life—the core set of attitudes, values and beliefs that shape the way we see life and respond to it.

Years of experience had given Florence the insight to recognize that she could choose to view life through the lens of anger or the lens of gratitude. The story of the man born blind also confronts us with a choice about two views of life. The Pharisees view life through the lens of the Mosaic Law, and that stance toward life blinds them to the good works Jesus performs and his identity in God. By contrast, the man born blind's experience of being healed changes his stance toward life. It gives his heart the lens it needs to recognize that Jesus is from God, and he becomes a disciple. To personalize the story of the man born blind, we need to explore these two stances toward life—these two different views of reality—in greater detail.

The Pharisees' stance toward life is centered on the Mosaic Law, and they view everything through that lens. This law-centered view of life causes them to focus on what the law requires and the punishments imposed on those who break it. Because the law dominates their attention, they interpret life from that perspective. God is viewed as the one who requires conformity to the law and punishes those who fail to measure up to its requirements. This view is static, steeped in the belief that the law was given once and for all by Moses. They view God's revelation as something in the past, and that view blinds them to the way in which God is present here and active now. Their law-centered view prevents them from seeing that the healing and reconciling ministry of Jesus is an extension of the presence of the liberating and redeeming God of Moses.

Jesus' stance toward life is fundamentally different from that of the Pharisees. He views life through the lens of God's kingdom and his own call to do God's work. While he values the Law of Moses, he sees the era of the law giving way to a new era in which God's healing and reconciliation are powerful, here-and-now realities. His view of life is characterized by a sense of urgency and a compelling mission to heal and reconcile. This view of life causes him to reach out immediately to heal the man born blind as well as others in need of healing and mercy. Because of this stance toward life, he is not about to let Sabbath rules or the law-based view of the Pharisees impede the mercy of God.

These two stances toward life are dramatically different, and they inevitably clash. That clash teaches us something about our own stances toward life. The Pharisees are sure that they are right. Their law-centered view blinds them to the healing ministry of Jesus, particularly its failure to conform to Sabbath rules. By overvaluing the Law of Moses, they discredit any information that conflicts with their view of life and fail to recognize that Jesus is from God. Whether they mean to do this or not is beside the point. Their stance toward life, like our own, causes them to see some things and be blind to others.

BLINDED BY DENIAL

The story of the man born blind also reveals a second way that we can experience blindness—denial. Denial is turning a blind eye toward something that will cause us pain, upset our world or force us to change. It often causes us to refuse to see what is right in front of our faces.

In the story of the man born blind, the dynamics of denial come to light near the end of the story. Throughout the story the authorities have gone to great lengths to make Jesus out to be a sinner. They fear that if they acknowledge that he has healed the man born blind, it will undermine their own positions of power and privilege. Jesus confronts them with a powerful statement: "I came into the world for judgment so that those who do not see may see and those who do see may become blind" (v. 39). The authorities express disbelief that Jesus could apply this statement to them: "Surely, we are not blind, are we?" (v. 40). Not only does their law-centered view of the world blind them, they are also blinded by denial. It is tempting to dismiss denial as an affliction of the Pharisees. Personalizing the story of the man born blind calls us to explore the dynamics of denial in our own lives.

Several years ago I was driving home from work. As I turned the corner at an intersection near my home, I noticed that the pavement was strewn with glass. I immediately recognized that a serious accident had occurred there. When I arrived at home, my wife Carla was not there. Since she often has late appointments, I paid little attention. As time passed, however, I grew more and more concerned. For all my worry, I never gave another thought to the glass on the road.

I had no luck reaching Carla on her cell phone or at her office. I called a friend who lived a block from her office, and asked her to check on Carla. No one was there, and her car was gone. I still didn't think of the glass on the road. It was another hour before I got the call from the hospital. She had been in the accident and was in the emergency room. I immediately knew where the accident had occurred. It was the first time in several anxious hours that I remembered the glass in the road. Thankfully,

Carla was not seriously injured. She had some painful bruises, but the X rays came back negative. She suffered no lasting injury.

This experience provides an example of denial-induced blindness. The pain of seeing is so great that we close our eyes and refuse to recognize something that is right in front of our face. I had seen the glass in the road and recognized that a serious accident had occurred. I was worried that Carla had been in an accident and was making phone calls to try to find out what had happened. Yet for some strange reason, I never put the pieces together. My physical sight was fine, but denial kept me from seeing.

Denial creeps into our lives in subtle ways. We are highly susceptible to it whenever we have our hearts set on something. We want it so badly that we become blind to any evidence that contradicts our ideal. When denial casts its spell on us, we may refuse to admit that the person we are crazy about might not feel the same way about us. We may fail to see ourselves in an accurate light and either inflate our strengths or exaggerate our flaws. We may fail to recognize a destructive pattern in our love relationships until it is deeply entrenched and has taken a serious toll.

As we personalize this story, we are invited to examine the patterns of denial in our own lives. As we recognize these patterns, we are called to open ourselves to Jesus' healing touch.

Jesus' Healing Touch

Jesus' touch has a remarkable power to heal and transform. In the story of the man born blind, we see how Jesus' touch heals the man's physical blindness, gives him the insight to recognize Jesus' identity in God and provides him with the courage to stand strong in the face of adversity. As we attempt to personalize this story in our own lives, we are invited to explore our own experience of Jesus' healing touch.

I changed schools at the start of third grade. On my first day in the new school, I encountered a crippled boy whose life has taught me much about Jesus' healing touch. It was impossible not to notice Tim—he came into class on crutches wearing a plaster cast on each leg. I later found out that he suffered from a congenital condition called arthrogryposis, which caused deformity in both his legs and his arms. On the day I first saw him, he was recovering from his usual summer routine—one or more serious surgeries.

While Tim's entrance into class captured my attention, it was nothing compared to what I experienced during recess. He became one team's quarterback in a pickup game of football. The game began with a rules discussion because Tim wanted to play tackle! Fortunately for everyone, less courageous players won the argument, and they played touch. The next obstacle was that the teams had no football. Tim immediately took the arm pad off one of his crutches, and it became the ball.

Picture in your mind's eye a seriously crippled third grader. Tim's at least a head shorter than anyone else on the field, and he's balanced on his crutches. He takes the snap from center and lofts a pass into the end zone for a touchdown. That scene repeated itself over and over during that recess and the ones that followed. Over the years it connected with other images to help me recognize that this kid with a crippled body had an amazing spirit and two defining characteristics: courage and character.

Tim and I have now known each other for almost five decades. Our long friendship has given me the opportunity to see how Jesus' healing touch has transformed his life. No, Tim didn't experience the kind of instantaneous healing that the man born blind did. There wasn't a single miraculous moment in which he put down his crutches and walked away healed. For Tim, Jesus' touch occurred over many years. It came to him in many ways, including the love of his remarkable parents.

Tim's parents loved him in two powerful ways. First, they raised him to be fiercely self-sufficient and independent. In nearly fifty years I've never seen him ask for slack or expect to be given any.

Second, they made it clear to him from a very early age that his future success depended on his mind. They knew that he would always face significant physical limitations, and they taught him to compensate by developing his mental abilities.

By the time Tim and I were in high school, he was walking independently. More importantly, his mental development was taking him toward a career in journalism. While I played second-string running back on our high school football team, Tim worked as a sportswriter covering the games—not for the school paper, but for the local daily. While I paid for college working jobs in bars, a convenience store and an oil refinery, he took his first editor's job at a weekly newspaper.

After Tim graduated from college, he went on to a career in journalism than spanned over thirty years. Always driven to excel, his career highlights include a long tenure as editor of the *Minneapolis Star Tribune*, working on committees to award the Pulitzer Prize and serving as president of the American Society of Newspaper Editors. At some point well into his career, Tim came to recognize the second dimension of Jesus' healing touch: Those who have been healed are also called to reach out and touch others. The crippled boy who had experienced Jesus' healing touch became a man who saw there was more at stake in his career than personal success. He came to recognize that his career was a calling, and that changed everything.

As a result of this second transformation, being an editor took on new meaning for Tim. It went beyond putting out an outstanding newspaper to include fostering values in the workplace and in his profession. Tim's strong convictions led him to use his positions of power and influence to urge others to recognize their roles in journalism as a calling, to commit themselves to excellence and to take up their responsibility to society. Today, Tim is deeply engaged in a second career that includes writing a nationally syndicated column on spirituality in the workplace, teaching and consulting on ethics and values, and serving as a lay preacher. He uses all of these avenues to encourage others to recognize their own calling and live it with conviction.[2]

Tim's life exhibits some remarkable parallels to the story of the man born blind. He received the healing touch of Jesus, and that touch led him to face adversity with courage and overcome difficult circumstances. Like the man born blind, Tim's experience of suffering, healing and transformation led him to recognize his call to discipleship. He now uses the many opportunities he has to witness to the calling in his own life and to encourage others to live their own lives as a calling.

Each of us is born into the painful limits of the human condition. Some of us—like my friend Tim and the man born blind—have physical infirmities that are immediately obvious. Others of us suffer from less visible wounds. We wrestle with inner wounds such as loneliness or depression, self-doubt or difficulty in loving ourselves, or the emotional scars left by past trauma. Whatever our experience of brokenness, our wounds invite us to open ourselves to the healing touch of Jesus. As we personalize the story of the man born blind, we are confronted with two critical questions. In what way have we received Jesus' healing touch? How has that touch called us to reach out and touch others?

Finding the Courage to Face Adversity

The man born blind finds himself in the midst of a fierce controversy. Jesus' mission of healing and reconciliation flies in the face of the law-based stance of the Pharisees, and the man born blind quickly becomes Exhibit A. Like it or not, the man is hauled onto center stage and provides an example of courage in the face of adversity. He clearly testifies to what has occurred, proclaims his belief that Jesus is from God, stands up to threats and accepts the consequence of his actions. The story gives disciples advice on how to respond to adversity.

Courage is a differentiator. Some of us have it, and others of us don't. The man born blind is in the first category. All too often I am in the second. My natural inclination is to avoid conflict. When I find myself in the midst of adversity, my tendency is to keep my head down and remain silent. If I do get drawn into the conflict, I usually try to assume the role of arbitrator or peacemaker. Claiming this role is an attempt to stay safe and above the fray. When I face the truth, I have to admit that I'm afraid of conflict.

Some years ago I was involved in negotiating a business agreement related to a start-up company in serious financial trouble. I was one of several people trying to keep the company afloat by restructuring both the company's debt and its ownership. At one point in the negotiation, my tendency to avoid conflict got the best of me. When the stakes were high and emotions were tense, I reluctantly agreed to some unfavorable terms. As a result, I was saddled with too much risk and not enough chance for an upside return.

After the deal was done, I was angry at myself and resentful of the terms I had agreed to accept. I stewed about it all that afternoon and evening. Then, I had a sleepless night. The next morning I got up early and did my usual workout. The exercise gave my anger an outlet, and I found myself peddling wildly on my stationary bike. Driven by my adrenaline, I peddled on and on while I had an angry conversation with myself. I knew I had made a bad deal. I didn't like the terms, but I had given my word. As I peddled on, the conversation continued. Finally, my feelings were vented enough for my anger to subside, and I started weighing my options. By the time I got off the bike, I knew what I had to do—even though I hated the thought of it.

That morning I went to see the person with whom I had made the agreement. I began by stating that I knew that we had an agreement and that I would honor the terms if he held me to them. I went on to say that I didn't think the deal was fair, and that I was angry at myself for making it. I stammered a lot in getting all this out, and eventually stumbled my way to the conclusion—that I wanted to reopen the negotiation. Needless to say, it was a very awkward meeting.

When I was finally finished, he was silent for what seemed like an eternity. I was squirming—both inside and out. Finally, he started laughing. Embarrassed and flustered, I demanded to know what he thought was so funny. He replied, "I'm usually the one who screws up and gets all bent out of shape. It's kind of funny to see you in that situation."

I shot back an angry: "You may think this is funny, but I hate it."

"I know," he said, "that's why I'm enjoying it so much." Then he laughed again. This time I laughed too. Then, we renegotiated the business deal on more acceptable terms. It wouldn't have happened if my anger hadn't given me the courage to stand up and do what I needed to do. It also wouldn't have happened if my colleague's fairness and integrity hadn't given him the willingness to renegotiate.

Personalizing the story of the man born blind invites us to look at how we deal with conflict and adversity. I'd like to assume that I would handle it like the man born blind, but the story makes it clear his parents didn't react that way. My own track record makes it hard to conclude that I would fare any better. As we try to find the courage to face adversity, we are forced to confront our fears. It is fear that paralyzes us when we are called to act. Acknowledging our fears helps us grasp that being courageous is not about being fearless. It's about being able to act in spite of our fears. The man born blind demonstrates this ability. As disciples we are called to do the same.

How Does This Story Call Me to Live?

As you try to make the story of Jesus healing the man born blind a part of your life, here are some questions to live and a suggestion for prayer.

Living the Questions

The following questions may help you live the story of Jesus healing the man born blind more fully.

• As I reflect on the story of Jesus healing the man born blind, what experiences in my life help me connect with the story?

• What is my experience of blindness? Is it physical, perceptual or spiritual?

• What is my stance toward life—the core attitudes, values and beliefs that shape the way I see life and respond to it?

• In what ways do I get blinded by denial, clinging to what is known and comfortable while being closed to what is surprising and new?

• What has been my experience of the healing touch of Jesus? In what way has that touch changed my life?

• How has my experience of the healing touch of Jesus called me to reach out and touch others?

Entering Into Prayer

Here is a suggestion for using the story of the man born blind as a way of entering into prayer:

Prayer for Insight and Awareness

The story of the man born blind is about seeing, not just seeing physically, but spiritually. This prayer is a way of reflecting on the events of my day and asking God for greater insight and self-awareness.

My life is busy—often too busy. Much of the time I am surrounded by a long list of things to do, people making demands on me and commitments that compete for my attention. In the midst of these pressures, I sometimes find it hard to think, much less to pray. When I most need the perspective that prayer provides, I often find myself struggling to find the time and space for it. That's when this prayer is most helpful to me.

This prayer involves looking back over the events of the day, so I usually use it as an "end of the day" prayer. The late evening invites me to prayer, and it prepares me for sleep.

Its structure is both simple and loose. For me, it usually involves four parts.

• I begin by quieting myself, breathing deeply, slowing down and letting go.

• Then I pray a simple prayer asking for the eyes to see how God has been with me during my day.

• I reflect on the events of the day, looking back on them to see what I missed as I was experiencing them. Often, this leads me to focus on one or more events that I now see in a different light.

> ★ Sometimes I become aware of a gift or blessing that I missed in the moment.

> ★ Other times I discover "second thoughts" and ponder things that I should have said or done.

★ This reflection often leads to insights or learning that I need to internalize.

★ My goal is to let the prayer lead me to the events in my day that reveal what I need to see.

• I conclude the prayer in whatever way is appropriate, depending on where the reflection has taken me.

★ Sometimes it's a prayer of gratitude for the gift or blessing that this reflection has helped me see.

★ Other times it's a prayer that asks forgiveness—either for something I did or for something I failed to do.

★ There is no set formula. The conclusion is a response to the experience of the prayer.

As you try this prayer, think of it as a discipline rather than an event. Using this prayer once may not be that helpful, but developing the habit of using it day after day has the potential to lead to new ways of seeing. Try it for a week, and see where it leads you.

CHAPTER FIVE

CONFRONTING STAGNATION AND DEATH
Jesus Raises Lazarus From the Dead (John 11:1–45)

WHAT'S THE EXPERIENCE OF THE STORY?

Setting the Scene

The conflict surrounding Jesus and his ministry continues to intensify, and Jerusalem is the center of the storm. He is attracting a significant following, and that threatens those in power. Jesus and the disciples are clearly aware of the danger they face. The cost of discipleship is becoming clear—it's a matter of life and death.

This story reaches its climax at Lazarus' tomb in the midst of his wake. The way different people respond as the story unfolds is striking. Martha wants to believe, but her practical side gets in the way. Mary kneels at Jesus' feet in a gesture of surrender. Some who witness Jesus raising Lazarus choose to believe in him. Others witness the same event and join the conspiracy to put him to death.

The story of Lazarus is a story within a story. John tells the story of Jesus raising Lazarus from the dead against the backdrop of the larger story of his entire Gospel—the story of whether the people who witness Jesus' signs choose to believe in him. The larger story confronts us with a fundamental choice: Do we believe in Jesus? The Lazarus story itself confronts us with a more specific dimension of that choice: Do we embrace Jesus as the resurrection and the life? Do we believe that he is with us in the many ways we experience dying? Will we entrust ourselves to his life-giving power?

Reading the Gospel

Read the story of Jesus raising Lazarus: John 11:1–45.

Retelling the Story

The story begins with Lazarus's illness, an illness serious enough that his sisters turn to Jesus for help. The message that Mary and Martha send demonstrates both how desperate they perceive the situation to be and how close their relationship with Jesus is: "Lord, he whom you love is ill" (v. 3). Jesus cannot fail to grasp the urgency of their request: Come at once, we need your healing power.

Jesus' response to the sisters' message conveys the theme of the story: "This illness does not lead to death; rather it is for God's glory so that the Son of God may be glorified through it" (v. 4). John's Gospel portrays Jesus as clearly in control, orchestrating the way events unfold. As John tells this story, Jesus knows immediately what will happen and how he will respond. In spite of his love for Lazarus and his sisters, Jesus appears to ignore their request and continue his work. He lets Lazarus's illness run its course—for God's glory and so that the Son of God may be glorified.

Two days later Jesus announces to the disciples that they are going to Lazarus's hometown of Bethany. The disciples can't believe it. They are fully aware of the danger that awaits them, and they respond by trying to reason with Jesus. "Rabbi, the Jews were just now trying to stone you, and are you going there again?" (v. 8). In effect, they are saying to Jesus: "You must be out of your mind." For Jesus, doing the work of God is more important than playing it safe. He explains that Lazarus has fallen asleep, and he is going to awaken him. The disciples are slow to understand what Jesus means and search for rationales to avoid the danger of going to Jerusalem. Jesus makes clear that Lazarus is dead and that they are going to Bethany. Fully grasping the danger, Thomas puts his life on the line and urges the others to do likewise: "Let us go that we may die with him" (v. 16).

Jesus and his disciples arrive in Bethany during the extended wake for Lazarus. He has already been entombed for four days, and the house is full of mourners from Jerusalem. Martha comes to meet Jesus even before he reaches the house. Her greeting is filled with emotion: "Lord, if you had been here, my brother would not have died" (v. 21). It must have been beyond her comprehension that Jesus did not arrive in time. This greeting may contain the frustration and disappointment of "What took you so long?" It may also be filled with the kind of anger and resentment that would cause us to ask, "Where in the world have you been?" We have no doubt that she is grief-stricken both by the loss of her brother and by Jesus' failure to prevent his death.

Above all, Martha is a practical woman. She may be grieving, but she also knows what she wants: "even now I know that God will give you whatever you ask..." (v. 22). The dialogue that follows between Martha and Jesus is revealing. Jesus first affirms, "Your brother will rise again" (v. 23). Martha indicates that she "knows that he will rise again in the resurrection on the last day" (v. 24). For Martha, the resurrection will happen—eventually. It is Jesus' next statement—"I am the resurrection and the life" (v. 25)—that Martha may not be ready to embrace. For Jesus, the resurrection is a "here-and-now" reality that he makes present. Even though Martha quickly affirms her belief in the resurrection, it won't be long before that belief is tested.

Martha leaves, goes to Mary and then sends her sister to Jesus. Mary kneels at his feet weeping and greets him with the same words that Martha did: "Lord, if you had been here, my brother would not have died" (v. 32). At this tender gesture of trust and surrender, Jesus "was greatly disturbed in spirit and deeply moved" (v. 33). He asks where Lazarus has been buried, and he weeps. His emotion provokes two reactions from those who witness it. Some are moved by his love for Lazarus. Others question why he could open the eyes of a blind man and not keep his friend from dying.

When Jesus reaches the tomb, he is once again moved deeply. He orders the stone taken away, and Martha can't help herself. She is so practical that she can't imagine Jesus knows what he's doing. "Lord, already there is a stench because he has been dead four days" (v. 39). Jesus' response—perhaps annoyed or even amused—chides her for her lack of faith. "Did I not tell you that if you believed you would see the glory of God?" (v. 40).

After the stone is rolled away, Jesus prays in gratitude that his prayer is always heard and "for the sake of the crowd" (v. 42). He then calls Lazarus out of the tomb with a loud voice. Martha and Mary must have held their breath, wondering whether Lazarus would respond. When Lazarus appears, he is bound with strips of cloth, and his face is wrapped. Jesus issues a command to free him— and all of us—from the power of death: "Unbind him, and let him go" (v. 44).

How Does the Story Touch Me?

As I reflect on how the story of Jesus raising Lazarus touches my life, there are several ways that I connect with it.

Grieving for a Loved One

I identify so strongly with Mary and Martha that this story stops me cold. Like them, I have lost a brother to death.

Mike was a Navy pilot flying combat missions over North Vietnam at the height of the war. For months I waited and worried. He was on the verge of returning home when his tour was extended. When he finally returned home safely after more than two hundred combat missions, I felt an enormous sense of relief. As a result, I was totally unprepared when he was killed in a crash during a training flight.

The first days after the accident are still a blur. Even in my memory, I view them through a haze of grief and tears. As the real-ity of Mike's death sank in during the months that followed, I faced some very dark times. It was more than a time of grief; it was a cri-sis of faith. My view of God was too small to encompass the expe-rience of my brother's tragic death. I had powerful emotions that I couldn't handle and no way to make sense of what had happened. I felt something of what Mary and Martha must have felt when they sent an urgent message asking Jesus for help, and he had failed to show up.

Slowly, out of the grief and the darkness, a way of making some sense of the tragedy began to emerge. While this didn't lessen the loss, it somehow made the grief more bearable. My too-small image of God began to give way to a deeper, more profound understand-ing of tragedy and how God is present with us in the midst of it. In my darkness I learned something of how Jesus is the resurrection and the life.

Mike was a pilot, and he loved to fly. God created him to be free and gave him the ability to choose. He knew the risks of flying and made the judgment that they were worth taking. In making that choice, he exercised his freedom. Unfortunately, the human condi-tion is flawed. As a result, the inevitable consequence of taking risks is that some of those risks end in tragedy. Sadly, that was the case with Mike's last flight. God doesn't want these tragedies to happen any more than we do. But the only way that God could prevent them would be to rob us of our freedom. Without our freedom, we could not choose love over hate, generosity over selfishness or life over death.

Mike's death shattered my too-small image of God. Yet God did not abandon me. Like Martha and Mary, the death of my brother caused me to encounter Jesus as the resurrection and the life in a deeper and more profound way. Out of the ashes of the crash, I have experienced something of the power of the resurrection. The God of resurrection and life is with us in the midst of tragedy, helping us rebuild our lives out of the broken pieces. Because God's faithfulness is more powerful than death, it calls us to resurrection, to a deeper and more profound life that we can only experience by passing through death.

Being Moved to Tears

When Jesus encounters Mary, she kneels at his feet and utters the same greeting that Martha did: "Lord, if you had been here, my brother would not have died." (v. 32). Jesus' response to Mary is filled with tenderness and emotion. "When Jesus saw her weeping, and the Jews who came with her also weeping, he was greatly disturbed in spirit and deeply moved" (v. 33).

In this response, we see the profound way that God is with us in our grief and pain. Jesus is touched to the depth of his being. He is cut to the heart, groans deeply and is moved to tears. This is the essence of the Incarnation. In Jesus God becomes fully human— entering into the depth of Mary's grief and weeping with those who are gathered. In this tender scene we experience the compassion of God embracing us in the midst of our suffering. At Lazarus's tomb Jesus reveals that God is with us in our deepest hurts, weeping with us.

When my father was in a coma and dying, I stood at his bedside with his mother. She was a stoic woman who had survived many tragedies, but this one was different. She was in great pain, and it is the only time I ever saw her weep. After a long time she turned to me and said, "If I could trade places with him, I'd do it in a minute." In that moment I grasped something of how God is with us in our grief. My father may not have even known his mother was there. Yet she was totally present with him—so present that she would have willingly taken his place in suffering and dying. That is the way that Jesus is present with Mary, Martha and the other mourners at Lazarus's tomb. His first response is not to act with power; it is to be present with those who weep. That is the way Jesus is present with us in the most painful moments of our life—whether we are aware of his presence or not.

Unlike Jesus, I find it hard to deal with grief and tears. I grew up as a survivor, and I've been socialized as a man. My modus operandi has more to do with numbness than with entering into the depth of life's painful experiences. I am comfortable with strength and helping; I find it hard to embrace vulnerability and emotion. When I'm caught in a tight spot emotionally—even if it's just a touching movie scene—I try to dry my eyes before the lights come up so that no one will notice. I feel the emotions deeply, but I'm not very comfortable with letting them show. My tears are frozen. When they start welling up, I stare into the distance, leave the room emotionally and numb out. Personalizing the story of Lazarus calls me to change. It calls me to be with those who grieve, to let the tears flow and to trust that the God who weeps can bring new life out of death—even the death of those we love so dearly.

Facing Martha's Challenge

In personalizing this story I face Martha's challenge: not letting my pragmatism block the ways that God brings life out of death. Although Martha must have been overjoyed when Lazarus emerged from the tomb, it was an embarrassing day. First, she makes a bold request—telling Jesus what she wants: "even now I know that God will give you whatever you ask…" (v. 22). When he questions her about her faith, she confidently professes her belief in the resurrection. Within minutes Jesus begins to fulfill her request, asking that the stone be rolled back from the tomb. Yet Martha's pragmatism overpowers her belief, and she tries to stop him: "Lord, already there is a stench because he has been dead four days" (v. 40).

There is a huge part of me that identifies with Martha's pragmatism. My pragmatic, Martha-side would never think of rolling back the stone. This sensible side of me grasps the reality of death—with all its stench and decay. It knows how risky it is to open a grave. Better to grieve and mourn. Better to cling to the distant hope of being reunited with Lazarus on the last day. Anything is better than facing the darkness of the tomb.

There is nothing wrong with pragmatism, as long as it doesn't become our dominant response to life. When pragmatism begins to take over, it squeezes out faith. I know about pragmatism because I make my living as a management consultant. In that role I advocate a clear game plan—spell out the action steps, set deadlines and clarify accountabilities. Unfortunately, life is by nature unpredictable. It doesn't unfold according to the plans we've made, and it can't be reduced to a simple formula or set of steps. There's more to it than that. To appreciate the "something more," we have to enter into the realm of faith and mystery. It is a realm that children embrace naturally. My grandchildren are relatively unimpressed by my credentials as a management consultant. What's important to them is whether I can enter into their experience. To do so, I have to temper my pragmatic instincts. It doesn't matter to them how many times they've played their favorite game—they want to play it again. Danielle doesn't really care how other kids play hide-and-seek, she enjoys hiding in the same place every time. For her, the high point of the game is the laughter and delight of being found.

To enter into the realm of mystery and faith, we have to leave our Martha-like pragmatism behind. Only then can we enter the realm of Danielle's laughter, beautiful sunsets and falling in love. Only then can we open ourselves to a God who surprises us by transforming the stench and decay of our lives into the fullness of life.

By the end of that unforgettable day, one thing is clear to Martha the pragmatist: She is not in charge. Like many of us, she probably likes taking charge. She may even be good at it. But it is now totally clear to her that the mystery of life and the power of God are beyond her control. She sent an urgent plea for Jesus' help, but he chose the timing of his arrival. She urged him not to roll back the stone, but he wouldn't listen. Her faith in the resurrection—so mixed with doubt, hurt and disappointment—was challenged in a public and embarrassing way. Her too-small image of God was shattered to make room for a deeper and more profound grasp of Jesus as the resurrection and the life. Her attempt to keep her brother in the tomb failed, and she received him back alive and healthy.

As we enter into the experience of the Lazarus story, we face Martha's challenge. We are called to let go of our pragmatism and trust the realm of mystery and faith. To do so, we may have to endure both excruciating waits and embarrassing moments. Ultimately, our tears will be turned into joy.

Rediscovering Our Passion for Life

When I was working my way through college tending bar, one of the bartenders I worked with had a saying: "A rut is a grave with the ends kicked out." In my twenties I had little experience of such ruts. Now that I've lived more than fifty years, I've known my share of them. Something in the Lazarus story connects me with my experiences of ruts and stagnation. There is a place within each of us where we are more dead than alive. When we encounter these stagnant places, we are—like Lazarus—entombed.

For twenty years of my career, I worked hard to build a successful company. The consulting firm that began as my solo practice grew into a firm that became well established and had a solid reputation for serving its clients. For most of those two decades, I had "two jobs." One was serving my own clients, and the other one was providing strategic leadership for the consulting firm. By the time I had reached my late forties, it was clear to me that the success of the company had been purchased at a significant cost to my mental, emotional and spiritual well-being. The work that I had once loved was no longer fun. I was in a rut, and something had to change.

When I'm faced with stagnation, my first tendency is the same as Martha's. I am afraid to roll back the stone for fear of the stench. It took me a long time to realize that when stagnation engulfs me, it can be a gift in disguise. Over time I've discovered that my stagnation has a life-serving purpose. It directs my attention to the aspects of my life that need to change.

Our lives have a momentum that is difficult to overcome. When I was faced with stagnation in my career, there were forces in my life urging me to ignore my instincts and stay in my rut. Yet the stagnation forced me to examine my life in a deeper way. It was a powerful catalyst for change. I needed to learn to embrace the dying part of me that I was working so hard to avoid. That part of me possesses some deep wisdom about what's not right in my life.

Stagnation and death are an inevitable part of life. We'd like to maintain the naïve view that Christian faith insulates us from these realities, but it doesn't. Human life is an agonizing mix of bitter and sweet. The moon waxes and wanes, reaching fullness only a few nights each month. Success is only possible when failure is also part of the picture. We live in a world filled with darkness as well as sunlight, hate as well as love, evil as well as good, and death as well as life. If we are to embrace life, we have to embrace the whole of it.

Far from sheltering us from these painful realities, Christian faith places us fully in the midst of them. The good news is that we do not face them alone. Jesus, the compassionate one who wept at Lazarus's tomb, also meets us in the dull rut of our stagnation. He weeps for us, and then he calls us out of the tomb. He touches us with a power stronger than death and gifts us with resurrection faith. That faith gives us the courage to roll back the stone, face the stench and walk into the light.

The stagnation of my late forties led me to face difficult choices. Once I moved past the denial of "everything's fine," my first instinct was to make minor adjustments in the externals of my life. I tried hiring someone to manage the company, devoting less time to work and taking up hobbies I had neglected for years. These external changes did little to restore my vital energy. Something more fundamental was necessary.

I found myself longing for prayer and solitude, and this quiet led to some intense soul-searching. I came to realize that I needed an inside-out, fundamental change. I needed to reconnect with my deepest passions and leave behind the things that led to exhaustion rather than fulfillment.

Somewhere along the way, my soul searching led me to discover what I call "the regret test." When I face a choice about whether or not to commit myself to something, I ask this basic question: "If I die without doing this, will I regret it?" This test often helps me distinguish what is truly important from what fails to engage my passion.

The regret test has helped me make some important decisions in my life. I decided to sell the company that I had led for almost twenty years and return to a solo consulting practice. I chose to spend more time with my grown stepchildren and my grandchildren. I gave up years of excuses and procrastination, and I finally wrote this book.

Something in the Lazarus story connects us with the stagnant inner places where we are dying. Our fear urges us to cling to the darkness of the tomb. By contrast, Jesus calls us to leave these dull ruts of stagnation behind, walk back into the light and embrace the resurrection. If we believe, we will see ourselves journey through the desert of grief and tears to rediscover our passion for what is truly important. If we believe, we will see the dead ends and detours of our lives give way to revitalization and new life. If we believe, we will see our stagnation and despair become wellsprings of creativity and gardens of hope.

The closing scene of the movie *Papillon*[1] captures what's at stake in our life and death struggle with stagnation. After years of separation, Papillon (played by Steve McQueen) is reunited with his fellow prisoner Dega (played by Dustin Hoffman). They were both sentenced to life on Devil's Island and arrived there together. Early in their imprisonment, they attempted to escape together but were recaptured and tortured. The long imprisonment has broken Dega's spirit. When the two meet again, Dega's home is a small square of dirt that he refuses to leave. He has literally become a prisoner of his own fear, waving a machete wildly in the air to keep imaginary intruders from invading his "home."

Papillon is a sharp contrast to Dega. During his imprisonment, he has made repeated escape attempts. When each one failed, he was subjected to solitary confinement, torture and other severe punishments. Yet after years of failed attempts, he is still determined to escape. Not far from Dega's prison of fear, he has fashioned a raft out of coconuts. He watches over the cliff as the waves crash against the rocks that surround Devil's Island, trying to read the pattern of the waves. He is determined to hurl the raft over the cliff, dive into the water and make one final attempt to achieve his freedom.

Jesus goes to the tomb of Lazarus and calls him forth. When we are entombed in the ruts of our own stagnation, he also calls to us. We can, like Dega, remain prisoners of our fear and hide in the darkness of the tomb. Or, like Papillon, whose name is the French word for butterfly, we can take a leap of faith. That leap requires us to trust that each rut in our life is a cocoon rather than a tomb. It requires us to trust in the resurrection and to believe that the words Jesus spoke to Lazarus are also meant for us: Unbind him...Unbind her...Let them go free!

How Does This Story Call Me to Live?

As you try to make the story of Lazarus a part of your life, here are some questions to live and a prayer that invites you to embrace Jesus as the resurrection and the life.

Living the Questions

One or more of the following questions may help you to more fully live the story of Jesus raising Lazarus from the dead. When you find a question that touches you, whether it's one of these or one that surfaces in you, let it take you where you need to go.

• As I reflect on the story of Jesus raising Lazarus from the dead, what experiences in my own life help me to connect with the story?

• When have I, like Martha, been disappointed by God and found myself struggling to trust that God was there for me?

• Has my experience of death, particularly tragic death, ever forced me to come to grips with having a too-small image of God? If so, how did that experience change my view of and relationship with God?

• How is God calling me to enter into the deepest moments of life—whether to weep or to rejoice—and be present with others in those moments?

• Have I ever experienced ruts and stagnation in my life? If so, when? How did I respond?

• When have I found the courage to roll back the stone, walk back into the light and embrace the resurrection?

Entering Into Prayer

Reflecting on the story of Jesus raising Lazarus led me to this prayer:

PRAYER FOR RESURRECTION AND LIFE

Jesus, you are the resurrection and the life. You wept at the tomb of Lazarus, and you know the loss I feel for my loved ones who have died. I trust that you can transform death into new life, an unending life in your presence. Be with me in my grief and turn my tears into joy.

Jesus, you are the resurrection and the life. You were deeply moved by those mourning Lazarus. Gift me with compassion that I might enter into the deepest moments of life—whether to weep or to rejoice—and be present with others. When I am isolated, let me connect with those around me. Where I am numb, let my frozen tears melt so that my emotions may flow freely. Let me move beyond numbness and fear to embrace the fullness of life—even when it costs me. Help me to trust that you will gift me with the compassion of God.

Jesus, you are the resurrection and the life. As with Martha, my pragmatism can blind me to the powerful ways you bring life from death. Give me the faith to trust that resurrection is a here-and-now reality, not just something that will happen eventually. Let me see the ways that your life-giving power fills the world around me with new life.

Jesus, you are the resurrection and the life. You know all my stagnant places, the deep ruts that I have worn in my life. Sometimes I lose hope and cling to the darkness of these tombs. Give me the courage to trust that you are present— even where I am broken and stagnant—bringing life out of death, hope out of despair and joy out of grief. Let me surrender to you and open myself to transformation.

Jesus, you are the resurrection and the life. Help me to turn away from stagnation, despair and isolation to embrace the life you bring. I long for this, even though I am afraid. Like Dega, I am often a prisoner of my own fear. Give me the courage to trust in you, to take Papillon's leap of faith and to choose freedom and life.

Jesus, you are the resurrection and the life. Give me the courage to roll back the stone and respond to your voice when you call me from the grave. Free me from the chains of sin and death so that I am able to walk into the light. Bring me fully alive in you so that I may live for the glory of God. Let my entire life be a joyful hymn that gives you thanks and praise!

Jesus, you are the resurrection and the life. Help me to trust that on the day I am called across the canyon of death you will hold out your hand and guide me home. Give me the courage to trust that you will seek me out, call me by name and welcome me with outstretched arms.

CHAPTER SIX

A LOVE STRONGER THAN DEATH

Jesus' Passion and Death (Matthew 26:14—27: 66)

WHAT'S THE EXPERIENCE OF THE STORY?

Setting the Scene

The conflict between Jesus and the authorities reaches the boiling point in Jerusalem during the feast of Passover. The long-brewing storm now strikes with full force. Powerful forces collide: good and evil, love and betrayal, suffering and death.

As the story unfolds, Jesus experiences one moment of truth after another. Each one demands a choice and carries serious consequences. In Gethsemane fear drives faith to the breaking point. In that moment of truth Jesus surrenders to the will of the Father, Judas betrays him with a kiss, and the disciples flee in fear. When Jesus appears before Pilate, integrity and truth hang in the balance. Jesus stays faithful to his mission even when the cost is death. Pilate, by contrast, makes an expedient compromise in a cowardly attempt to salve his conscience and appease the crowd. Ultimately, Jesus gives his life in redemptive love—embracing the cross and staying faithful to death.

As we attempt to personalize the story of Jesus' passion and death, we follow him through his final hours. The story confronts us with the same choice that Jesus and the others faced. When we face the ultimate challenge, will we be able to embrace the cross in love?

Reading the Gospel

Read Matthew's account of Jesus' passion and death: Matthew 26:14—27:66.

Retelling the Story

Matthew's account of Jesus' passion begins with the disciples asking Jesus where he wants them to prepare the Passover (v. 17). For Matthew's Jewish audience Passover immediately establishes the themes of sacrificial death, deliverance and covenant. The first Passover in Egypt—and every one since—involved offering a lamb during a sacrificial meal. This time Jesus is the lamb of sacrifice. The first Passover delivered the people of Israel from their slavery in Egypt, and now Jesus delivers humankind from its slavery to sin. The first Passover initiated a covenant between God and Israel sealed in blood, and now Jesus seals a new covenant by pouring out his own blood on the cross.

In the face of betrayal and death, Jesus takes the bread, blesses it and gives it to his disciples. He is carrying out the Passover ritual until he transforms its meaning: "Take, eat; this is my body" (v. 26). Jesus builds on the richness of the Passover and redefines it with his own sacrifice. "Drink from it, all of you; for this is my blood of the covenant, which is poured out for many for the forgiveness of sins" (vv. 27–28). Jesus freely lays down his life in redemptive love; the new covenant is sealed with the blood of that sacrifice.

Jesus enters Gethsemane painfully aware of how alone he is. Judas will betray him, the disciples will abandon him, and Peter—for all his talk—will repeatedly deny him. In his aloneness Jesus turns to God in prayer. He asks most of the disciples to stay at a distance, and only Peter, James and John accompany him. Overcome with sadness, he speaks openly about it with the three: "I am deeply grieved, even to death" (v. 38). Jesus asks them to "remain here, and stay awake with me" (v. 38). Going off by himself, he falls on his face in prayerful surrender. "My Father, if it is possible, let this cup pass from me; yet not what I want but what you want" (v. 39).

When Jesus returns to his three closest disciples, they are asleep. He admonishes Peter: "So, could you not stay awake with me one hour?" (v. 40). His words provide powerful insight about the role of prayer in times of trial. "Stay awake and pray that you may not come into the time of trial; the spirit is indeed willing, but the flesh is weak" (v. 41).

This sequence of events repeats itself three times. Each time Jesus returns, the disciples are asleep. When he returns the third time, he knows his betrayer is arriving. "See, the hour is at hand, and the Son of Man is betrayed into the hands of sinners" (v. 45). He rouses his disciples: "Get up. Let us be going" (v. 46).

Judas arrives with an armed crowd. He approaches Jesus, greets him and in a bitter irony betrays him with a kiss. Jesus surrenders, but one of the disciples is determined to go down fighting. He draws his sword, strikes a servant and severs his ear. Jesus stops him: "Put your sword back into its place; for all who take the sword will perish by the sword" (v. 52). Jesus makes clear that he could summon legions of angels to rescue him but will not because "how then would the scriptures be fulfilled, which say it must happen in this way?" (v. 54). God will not make a diving catch to save Jesus from the forces of evil and the finality of death. Jesus is arrested, and the disciples flee into the night.

Jesus is led off to the high priest who has assembled his council, the Sanhedrin. One by one, witnesses come forward to testify against Jesus, but they fail to produce the evidence needed to put him to death. Through it all, Jesus remains silent. Finally, the high priest becomes frustrated and says to Jesus: "I put you under oath before the living God: tell us if you are the Messiah, the Son of God" (v. 63). Jesus now openly acknowledges his identity, knowing that by doing so he is surrendering his life.

> But, I tell you,
>   From now on you will see the Son of Man
>   seated at the right hand of the Power
>   and coming on the clouds of heaven. (v. 64)

Interpreting Jesus' revelation of his true identity as blasphemy, the high priest tears his clothes, saying: "He has blasphemed! Why do we still need witnesses?" (v. 65). He asks the members of the council for their opinion, and their answer is clear: "He deserves death" (v. 66).

Peter has followed Jesus at a distance. While Jesus is with the Sanhedrin, Peter is waiting in the courtyard with the servants, hoping to find out what happens. He is very much alone, and fear is getting the best of him. First a servant girl confronts him: "You also were with Jesus the Galilean" (v. 69). Peter denies it in front of all the servants: "I do not know what you are talking about" (v. 70). He is then confronted by a second servant girl, and later by other bystanders. With each accusation his denial gets stronger. Finally, he calls down curses on himself and swears: "I do not know the man!" (v. 74). As the cock crows, Peter remembers that Jesus predicted his denial. He goes out and weeps bitterly.

Peter is not the only one feeling remorse. When Judas finds out that Jesus has been condemned to death, he attempts to return the thirty pieces of silver to the authorities. "I have sinned by betraying innocent blood" (27:4). Judas throws the silver into the sanctuary and hangs himself in despair.

When Jesus is brought before Pilate, there's a new spin on the charges against him. The Sanhedrin has already found him guilty of blasphemy, but has no authority to issue the death sentence. As governor, Pilate has little interest in religious disputes, so blasphemy means nothing to him. When Jesus is arraigned before Pilate, he is accused of treason for claiming to be the king of the Jews. Treason is a charge that gets the governor's attention, something he can punish with death. If Jesus had been executed for blasphemy, he would have been stoned. Treason has a higher price: crucifixion.

Jesus isn't the first person Pilate has tried for treason. He governs a volatile territory where various factions advocate the overthrow of Rome. Pilate comes to the trial experienced in dealing with revolutionaries, and he expects to dispatch the matter quickly. From the first moment, however, Pilate's encounter with Jesus is anything but routine. In Pilate's experience revolutionaries come in two sizes. Most are "little ones" who lose their bravado as soon as they are arrested. By the time they appear before him, they grovel in an attempt to make any deal that will spare their miserable lives. A few "big ones" remain defiant, at least until the beatings start. Both sizes are sentenced quickly and without incident.

To Pilate's surprise, Jesus doesn't fit either mold. What first gets Pilate's attention is Jesus' composure. It's more than a steeled will refusing to let a volcano of emotion erupt. It's deeper than a resignation to his fate. What Pilate senses—whether he can name it or not—is the inner peace that Jesus possesses. There's something more, too. Pilate sees in Jesus' eyes something he has never before seen in the eyes of an accused man: a forgiving love. Ironically, it is the depth of Jesus' composure that most unnerves Pilate. As he confronts the deep calm of Jesus' love, he is shaken to the core.

Integrity hangs in the balance during Pilate's encounter with Jesus. The accused stays true to his identity, willing to pay the ransom evil demands. Jesus refuses to deny his relationship with God or compromise his mission in order to save his skin. The judge, by contrast, is caught between the rock of his conscience and the hard place of a demanding crowd. Pilate is a crafty survivor, and he pushes against the rock trying to find an expedient solution. First, he attempts to use a custom of the festival to release Jesus, but he misreads the crowd. They want Barabbas, a notorious criminal imprisoned with rioters who committed murder during an uprising. The first outcome of Pilate's expedience is ironic: He continues to try a man who he believes is innocent while trying to appease the crowd by releasing a known insurrectionist.

The situation continues to deteriorate. Jesus is caught in the middle of a bargaining session between Pilate and the crowd. Integrity was the first casualty, and now responsibility becomes the second. Pilate is the only one with the authority to pronounce sentence on Jesus, yet he attempts to blame the crowd for the outcome. His public hand washing is a dramatic portrayal of refusing to accept responsibility and looking for someone to blame.

Hours of unspeakable torture and suffering follow, leading to Jesus' death. In addition to scourging Jesus, the soldiers strip him of his clothes and crown him with thorns. Finally, they dress him in his own clothes and lead him off to crucifixion. As Jesus drags his cross toward Golgotha, the soldiers get impatient. They want to get this thing over with as quickly as possible, and Jesus is slow and stumbling. One of them scans the crowd and—who knows why—his eyes land on Simon of Cyrene. It's doubtful he volunteered for the assignment. As the crowd passed, he probably edged forward to get a glimpse of what was happening. The next thing he knows, the soldiers are forcing him to carry someone else's cross.

When they reach Golgotha, the soldiers crucify Jesus, placing the charge against him over his head: "This is Jesus, King of the Jews" (v. 37). As Jesus' torn and broken body hangs from the cross, darkness covers the earth. He experiences a death of unspeakable pain. He tastes the death of being alone—abandoned by his followers and deserted by his friends. He touches the death of doubt and uncertainty, wondering whether his mission will succeed and whether his followers will carry on without him. He feels the death of waiting, one breath at a time, not knowing how many are left. As Jesus hangs from the cross, he sees his lifeblood is draining away and knows that death is near. Through it all, his love never falters.

Near the end Jesus cries out, "My God, my God, why have you forsaken me?" (v. 46). These are not words of despair; they are the opening words of Psalm 22. Jesus' prayer from the cross is a psalm expressing his confidence that God never fails to deliver those in distress. Finally, he cries out in a loud voice and gives up his spirit.

At the moment of Jesus' death, the centurion and the other soldiers guarding Jesus witness all that is taking place, and they are terrified. Their fear moves them to belief, and they exclaim, "Truly, this was God's Son" (v. 54). The women who "had followed Jesus from Galilee and had provided for him" (v. 55) watch all this from a distance. In the evening Joseph of Arimathaea goes to Pilate and requests Jesus' body. He wraps it in a shroud, puts it in his own new tomb and rolls a stone across the entrance. "Mary Magdalene and the other Mary were there, sitting opposite the tomb" (v. 61).

HOW DOES THE STORY TOUCH ME?

As I reflect on how the story of Jesus' passion and death touches my life, here are some of the ways that I connect with the experience of the story.

Gethsemane: Faith at the Breaking Point

Jesus' experience in Gethsemane demonstrates how fear pushes faith to the breaking point. In the garden he confronts his fear of suffering and death. The cost of surrendering to the Father's will is clear, and he chooses to pay the price. Because his trust in God is stronger than his fear of death, Jesus chooses to stay faithful to God and true to his mission even when the price of fidelity is suffering and death.

In Gethsemane fear also pushes the disciples' faith to the breaking point. The spirit is willing, but the flesh is weak. In contrast to Jesus, their fear proves stronger than their faith. They abandon Jesus and flee to save their skins. Even Peter—the one so sure of his courage—repeatedly denies Jesus, swearing an oath that he doesn't know him. As we personalize the story of Jesus' passion and death, we come face to face with the Gethsemanes in our own lives, those times when fear pushes our faith to the breaking point.

Steven Speilberg's movie *Saving Private Ryan*[1] is based on the true story of U.S. Army Rangers behind enemy lines in World War II. Their mission is to find a soldier whose three brothers have all been killed in action and return him home safely. They display amazing courage and resourcefulness in carrying out their mission. By contrast, in a crucial battle, we see the agonizing struggle of Corporal Upham (played by Jeremy Davies)—a young soldier completely immobilized by fear. His spirit may be willing, but his flesh is weak. Like the disciples in Gethsemane, he hides from the action in order to save his skin. His failure to deliver ammunition to those under fire results in the death of two other soldiers.

Several years ago I signed up for what I thought would be a nice weekend of personal growth. Unexpectedly, it landed me in Gethsemane face to face with my fear. Like the soldier Spielberg portrays, I found myself paralyzed. Ironically, it wasn't in the heat of battle, it was in the process of trying to build community.

After reading the book *A Different Drum*[2] by M. Scott Peck, I decided to attend a weekend of community building led by facilitators from the Foundation for Community Encouragement. A group of approximately twenty-five people—almost all of us strangers to one another—gathered at a retreat house in Northern Michigan. Our goal was to build community during a two-day experience. I was hoping to both experience community and learn something about how to build it.

The weekend began simply enough—each of us talking about why we came and what we hoped to gain from the experience. But, as you'd expect, the road from twenty-five strangers to being a community had a few potholes in it. To be honest about it, for me one of those potholes was the approximate size of the Grand Canyon. As we attempted to become a community, our various expectations and agendas begin to collide. Peck refers to this as "chaos," and I'd say it's a pretty good description—both of what was going on in the group and what was happening in my stomach. Trying to move beyond chaos is what put me in Gethsemane.

According to Peck, there are only two ways that a group can move beyond chaos. One way is to try to "get organized" and attempt to manage the chaos. Unfortunately, getting organized prevents the group from becoming a community. My head did a good job of coaching me not to fall into the trap of trying to get organized. All right, if I'm really honest, I did offer a suggestion or two. But I didn't push too hard. My Gethsemane dilemma had to do with the other option.

Peck describes the other way to move beyond chaos as *emptying*. Emptying is the only path toward community. I was clear enough about emptying in my head; I'm sure I could have given the book report. Unfortunately, the group I was with didn't seem too interested in a book report. They were expressing intense feelings: hurt, anger, grief—the whole rainbow of emotion and vulnerability. I had some of these feelings too. It's just that I was trying to have them without anyone noticing it. I was hoping to have my chaos in private, while I helped other people deal with theirs.

In Gethsemane Jesus trusts God enough to empty himself. He moves beyond his fear, lets go of his own agenda, opens himself to whatever comes and surrenders to God. What I did that weekend was let my fear get the best of me. I pretty much flunked "Emptying 101." I flunked it the same way the disciples did—by running away. My body never left the room, but I had an out-of-body experience. Mentally and emotionally, I got out of Dodge.

By the time the weekend concluded, many of the people had experienced community. For my part, I had seen something of what it takes to build community, but my inability to act in the face of my fear kept me from being fully a part of it. Through my struggle, however, I had learned how much I needed to go to "emptying school." As we personalize the story of Jesus' experience in Gethsemane, we become more deeply aware of the Gethsemane moments in our own lives. These moments invite us to empty ourselves, claim a faith more powerful than our fear and trust God enough to surrender.

Jesus Before Pilate: The Price of Integrity

Jesus' appearance before Pilate demonstrates the price of integrity. He stays true to his identity as the Son of God even when the cost is suffering. He remains faithful to his mission of redemption even when the price is death. I know something of the price of integrity, and I bet you do too. Sometimes I've been willing to pay it, and other times I've failed to ante up.

Pilate's behavior—and the ways my own is similar—reminds me of a piece of wisdom that my Uncle Mert once passed on to me: People are like electrons; they follow the path of least resistance. During Jesus' trial Pilate is an electron desperate to find an easier way, and he chooses the path of expedience. When integrity and responsibility are at stake, Jesus makes it clear that we have a choice. We are called to be more than electrons—even when the price of that choice leads to the cross.

The stage play *Les Miserables*[3] provides a dramatic example of choosing integrity over expedience. The main character is Jean Valjean, escaped prisoner 24601. Transformed by a generous act of mercy, Valjean has lived an exemplary life for years. All that time, a police lieutenant named Javier has continued to pursue him. At one point Valjean learns that a man believed to be prisoner 24601 is on trial, threatened with being returned to prison. If this man is found guilty, Valjean's freedom is assured. He could choose the path of least resistance, keep his mouth shut and let the other man go to prison in his place. Valjean decides to be more than an electron, chooses the way of integrity and voluntarily reveals that he is prisoner 24601 in order to free the other man.

Several years ago the consulting industry I work in experienced a significant downturn. During those "bad times," I secured a new client whose business was growing rapidly. Early in the consulting engagement, however, I learned that my new client had some questionable business practices. As I was thinking through whether to resign the account, I sought the advice of a colleague whom I trust both for his moral sense and his business judgment. After listening to my story, he summed up the dilemma in one sentence: "So you're asking me if the shaky financial condition of the company is sufficient justification for you to continue to do business with a client that compromises your ethical integrity." I laughed out loud, knowing that his summation was exactly right. Every one of my rationalizations had hedged the issue; he had cut to the core of it. I responded with a feeble: "Not if you put it like that…" He paused for a minute to let me think. Then, with genuine sympathy, he asked, "How else would you put it?"

Thoreau once wrote, "There are a thousand hacking at the branches of evil to one who is striking at the root."[4] My colleague's keen moral sense and his detachment from the situation gave him the perspective to strike at the root. His bald framing of the issue made the answer clear, and it helped me quit hacking at the branches. I resigned the account.

Personalizing Jesus' encounter with Pilate encourages us to examine how we handle the choice between expedience and integrity. It gives us a moral compass to recognize the situations that put our integrity at risk. Choosing integrity takes the kind of courage that Jean Valjean demonstrates by risking imprisonment to spare another man. It takes accepting responsibility for our actions rather than adopting Pilate's attempt to wash the guilt from his hands by blaming someone else. Choosing integrity takes the kind of prayerful surrender to God's will that Jesus demonstrates—trusting that no amount of suffering or even death has the power to separate us from the love of God.

Choosing the Cross

As we personalize Jesus' decision to take up his cross, we are confronted with three responses to carrying it. Like the disciples, we can refuse the cross and run away. Like Simon of Cyrene, we can carry the cross because it's forced on us. Or, like Jesus, we can willingly embrace it.

The disciples are called to embrace the cross, but it is too much for them. They refuse it and flee into the night. Peter goes even further, trying to lie his way out of a tight spot. When we are confronted with the cross, sometimes it is too much for us. Like the disciples, we refuse to have any part of it. My friend Nadine provides a dramatic example of refusing the cross. She gave Christianity a good, hard look and decided not to commit. I once asked her what led to her decision, and she gave me an insightful response: "I've read the Gospels, and I know that Christians are called to take up Jesus' cross. But the cross is suffering and death." Then, making the Sign of the Cross for emphasis, she concluded, "I'm not about to lay the cross on myself." In refusing the cross, Nadine joins the disciples in running away. I know how she feels, and I bet you do too. When I confront the cross, I sometimes run away.

Refusing the cross doesn't have to be as dramatic as the disciples' flight or as unequivocal as Nadine's refusal to commit. If we are honest with ourselves, we are forced to acknowledge the ways we refuse the cross every day. We refuse it when we look for the easy way out, fail to respond to someone in need or close our eyes to injustice. We refuse it when we nurse resentments about the burdens others place on us or whine about life's unfairness. We refuse the cross when we force our way to the head of the line, finesse situations to get our own way or make subtle compromises to keep our lives comfortable. We refuse it when we avoid the awkwardness of surfacing a tough issue that no one wants to face or pack our lives so full of "other priorities" that we don't have time for prayer.

Simon of Cyrene represents a second response to the cross: shouldering it because he has no choice. He finds himself in the wrong place at the wrong time. What alternative did he have? There's no arguing with a centurion and his men. Being fair has nothing to do with it. Simon had little choice, and sometimes we don't either. Life doesn't hand out hardship and pain in equal shares. Some of us get more than our share while others appear to get off easy. No matter what cards we get dealt, we have to play the hand. Simon gets dealt a tough hand, but he still has an option. Granted, he doesn't have much choice about whether to shoulder the cross. Resisting the soldiers' attempt to conscript him would have cost him dearly. What Simon can choose, however, is the attitude he takes toward carrying it.

When my Uncle Leo was suffering with cancer, he reached that awful point when all the treatment options had been exhausted. He was dying, and he knew it. The only thing that the doctors could do was help make him comfortable. The only thing Leo could do was make the most of the time he had. Just as Simon was dragged from the crowd and forced to carry Jesus' cross, Leo was forced to bear the cross of a painful death to cancer.

Even when a cross is forced upon us, we have a choice about how we respond to it. During his last days, Leo chose—with his mind, his heart and his will—to live with dignity. He rarely mentioned his pain or complained about his circumstances. If he felt bitter "why me" kinds of resentments, I never heard him express them.

He took the time to be with and appreciate those he loved, spending special moments with each of us. When he talked about his life, it was with a sense of gratitude. In those days Leo taught me that even when a cross is forced on us, we can choose the attitude we have toward it. He didn't choose to die, but he made powerful choices about the way he lived his final days.

Jesus demonstrates the third response to the cross—willingly embracing it. It's not that he doesn't hesitate. We've already seen how he hesitates in Gethsemane. We're not the only ones with doubts and second thoughts. Perhaps they are inevitable, embedded somehow in our DNA. We experience buyer's nerves the night before we close on our first house. We find ourselves staring out the window two days before our wedding asking: *until death, am I sure?* Just before he puts his life on the line, Jesus hesitates too. What's important, though, is what happens next. When he hesitates, Jesus gathers himself in prayer, surrenders to God and puts it all on the line. What counts is that once he commits, he never looks back.

Arland Williams, Jr., never looked back. On the morning of January 13, 1982, National Airport in Washington, D.C., was closed by a blizzard. Shortly after it reopened, Williams boarded Air Florida Flight 90 to Tampa. The plane was delayed at the gate after deicing and then waited in line before takeoff. By the time it attempted to take off, ice had formed on the wings and also prevented the engines from achieving sufficient power for takeoff. The plane stalled before it reached an altitude of five-hundred feet, crashed into the 14th Street Bridge and ended up in the icy waters of the Potomac River.

Williams found himself in the freezing water with five other survivors. Bystanders and news crews watched from the shore, completely helpless. A park police helicopter trailing a lifeline finally reached those in the water. When the rope came to Williams, he passed it to one of the other survivors. The helicopter returned after that rescue, and Williams again passed the rope to another survivor. By the time the helicopter returned for the last rescue, he had drowned.[5]

Arland Williams, Jr., willingly sacrificed his own life. He embraced death so that others could live. In unexpected and tragic circumstances, he opted to save others when his own life was on the line. On the edge of death, he made the choice to pass the rope.

Embracing the cross requires paying the ultimate price: surrendering our own lives so that others may live. Jesus made that choice in Gethsemane, and Arland Williams, Jr., made it in the icy waters of the Potomac. Every day, we choose whether or not to put others ahead of ourselves in small ways. For some of us the day will come when we will face the ultimate choice. On that day we can cling to the rope, or we can embrace the cross by passing the rope so that someone else will live.

A Love That Never Fails

As I try to connect with the experience of Jesus' passion and death, my mind's eye pictures Jesus hanging from the cross. It's an amazing act of love. As my awareness of that image deepens, I learn more of the experience of the cross and the way it calls me to give myself in love.

It's mid-morning, and I'm doing what I do—leading a strategy formulation retreat for a corporate client. Surrounded by a group of fifteen executives, I get a sudden glimpse of Jesus hanging on the cross. The air is thick with fear as they talk about the company's poor performance. Egos are threatened, and the blame game is raging out of control. Those with the most power are wielding it while those with less seem divided into two camps—one silent and the other making excuses. I realize that Jesus isn't the only one hanging from the cross.

One guy launches an attempt to hijack the meeting, and I feel a toxic bile churning in my stomach. As a few willing accomplices join him, a voice in my head screams, "Get the worms back in the can!" That image—Jesus hanging from the cross—stays with me. What is that redemptive love asking of me? In my anger and frustration I fight two competing instincts: Part of me wants to plant my fist in someone's face, and another part of me wants to run screaming from the room. Jesus' love holds me fast. Somehow, that image—that connection with Jesus on the cross—helps me find my way. I take one breath at a time and resist the instinct to take control. Someone begins an attack on me for letting the group founder, and I swallow hard. I fight the urge to launch a counterattack, and I struggle to empty myself. The image of Jesus deepens into a silent prayer, but I'm not sure it will be enough.

Time seems to stand still, much like it must have for Jesus on the cross. Ever so slowly, I sense a subtle shift as the comments contain less venom. The attacks subside, and the tide begins to turn. A woman who has been silent for most of the morning finds her voice. She does what no one else has: She risks speaking openly about her own feelings and names the fear in the room. I breathe a grateful sigh, wondering if she also pictures Jesus on the cross. Her emptying has a redemptive effect. Several others find their voices, and they also speak in the first person. Their vulnerability lets the emptying continue. Slowly, it clears a space where something new can begin to happen. The executives confront the reality that their company may be dying. As they find the courage to name that reality, the right discussion begins. The fear starts to give way to determination. The group launches—tentatively—the painful task of working together to find another path. The company's future—and their own—is far from assured, but the odds are starting to improve.

That image of Jesus hanging on the cross helps me confront the ways that I am dying. As I see the life drain out of him, it helps me connect with the ways that I am called to love deeply enough to embrace death so that others may live. I am called to die by letting go of my agenda—my definitive plan for how life should work—and opening myself to ideas and suggestions of others. I am called to die by listening deeply to others rather than asserting my position or planning my rebuttal. I am called to die by keeping my ego in check when I want to lash out at others or win at all costs. I am called to die by giving up my preoccupation with appearances and what people think so that I can do the right thing when it's neither cool nor popular. I am called to die by surrendering in prayer when I'd rather maintain control and call my own shots.

As we attempt to personalize the experience of Jesus on the cross, we begin to realize that crosses—and the invitations to love that they embody—come in all shapes and sizes. We experience little ones that invite us to connect with Jesus' passion every day. It's the small cross of taking the time to seriously consider a contrary point of view when our minds are already made up. It's the emptying required to derail our efforts to complete our lists of things to do when a child or a friend needs time with us. It's taking the risk of naming the elephant in the room or raising an ethical question when these could be career-limiting moves. It's making room in our lives when we unexpectedly cross paths with someone in need. It's struggling to stay patient and open to someone who needs our time and attention when we're fed up with life and running on empty.

The more deeply we reflect on the image of Jesus on the cross, the more of these invitations to love that we will recognize. By choosing to die in little ways each day, we create the habits of love that shape our lives. We go to emptying school and learn to surrender. Developing this discipline in our lives prepares us for the moment in our lives when we will be called to love enough to risk it all. We never know when we might find ourselves in the icy waters reaching for a lifeline and confronting a choice. Someday, the doctor may look at us with a solemn face, deliver bad news and force us to choose how we will approach death. On that day we will be called to embrace the cross in love and stay faithful until death. In that moment, which is both our ultimate challenge and our finest hour, we will be called to let go of our lives and fall into the welcoming arms of the God whose love is stronger than death.

How Does This Story Call Me to Live?

As you try to make the story of Jesus' passion and death a part of your life, here are some questions to live and a suggestion for prayer.

Living the Questions

One or more of the following questions may help you live the story of Jesus' passion and death more fully.

- As I reflect on the story of Jesus' passion and death, what experiences in my own life help me to connect with the story?

- When I face Gethsemane moments in my own life, how do I respond? Am I able—like Jesus—to trust God enough to surrender? Or like the disciples, do I run away to save my skin?

- When Jesus encounters Pilate, he demonstrates that he is willing to pay the price that integrity demands. When have I faced an ethical dilemma and been forced to make a choice? In what ways did I try to rationalize my way out of the situation?

- Who are the people in my life that I trust enough to consult for ethical guidance? When I need a moral compass, to whom could I turn?

- When I face the choice of whether to take up my cross, what is my response? Do I respond like the disciples, Simon of Cyrene or Jesus?

- In what ways does my image of Jesus hanging on the cross help me connect to my everyday experiences of the cross? How does my mental image keep me focused in times of suffering?

Entering Into Prayer

GETHSEMANE PRAYER

This suggestion for prayer is based on Jesus' Gethsemane experience and his prayer of surrender. In Gethsemane Jesus is torn and deeply conflicted. He knows that being faithful to his mission and true to his relationship with the Father has a huge price—suffering and death. Part of him knows what he is called to do, but another part of him is fighting it.

- Begin your prayer with a brief quieting prayer. Either make up your own or use the one in chapter eight, pp. 133–135.

- Once you have quieted yourself, slowly read Matthew's account of Jesus in Gethsemane: Matthew 26:36–46.

- As you reflect on that Scripture passage, take time to identify ways that you —like Jesus—wrestle with God's call. One or more of the following questions may help you in that reflection.

  * As you reflect on Jesus' Gethsemane experience, what situations that you are facing come to mind?

  * In what ways do you find yourself confronting choices you don't want to make?

- ⋆ What are the situations in which you are torn and ambivalent—part of you wanting to do God's will while another part of you is trying to avoid it?

- ⋆ What are the situations in which your spirit is willing but your flesh is weak?

- ⋆ What is God asking of you that you'd rather not give?

- Once you have become aware of some of the ways you connect with Jesus' experience of Gethsemane, begin to use the words of Jesus' Gethsemane prayer:

  > "My Father, if this cup cannot pass by
  > without my drinking it, your will be done."

- Bring each situation to mind and pray Jesus' words in response. Here's an example:

  > I find myself resisting time for prayer, and I
  > distract myself by staying busy with unimportant things...
  > "My Father, if this cup cannot pass by
  > without my drinking it, your will be done."

- Continue this prayer, like you would pray a litany, until you have brought each situation before God and prayed Jesus' words in response.

- Conclude your prayer by asking God for the help you need to surrender.

Consider repeating this prayer every day for a week. The repetition will deepen your awareness of the ways you are resisting God and give you the opportunity to surrender in prayer.

CHAPTER SEVEN
SURPRISED BY THE GOD OF EASTER
Jesus Is Raised From the Dead (Matthew 28:1–10)

WHAT'S THE EXPERIENCE OF THE STORY?

Setting the Scene

This story begins where the story of the passion ended—at Jesus' tomb. The end becomes a new beginning. The faithful women who were with Jesus at the cross are surprised by amazing events as new life bursts forth from the place of death. For those of us accustomed to experiencing Good Friday confident that the resurrection will follow quickly, it is hard to imagine the overwhelming impact of that first Easter. Nothing has prepared the women for this moment.

The scene at the tomb is in dramatic contrast to the same scene at the end of the last story. The stone was placed over the entrance to the tomb under the shadow of Jesus' death and the darkness of night. Now that darkness is chased away by dawn and the dazzling light of an angel's presence. The God who seemed absent during the crucifixion is now revealed in the power of an earthquake and presence of the angel. The stone that symbolized the finality of Jesus' burial is now rolled away, and the empty tomb becomes a dramatic sign that Jesus is risen.

As the women lead us to the tomb and a new day dawns, the earth isn't the only thing that shakes. Everything in us—from the way we view death to our experience of God—is shaken to the core. With the women, we are called to look into the empty tomb, trust the resurrection and surrender to Easter's life-giving power.

Reading the Gospel

Read Matthew's account of Jesus' resurrection: Matthew 28:1–10.

Retelling the Story

Mary Magdalene and her friend Mary start out for Jesus' tomb before dawn. Light is just beginning to gather on the horizon, but it is still more night than day. Since Jesus' suffering and death, grief has allowed them little sleep. Every time they close their eyes, horrible images of his broken and bleeding body flood in on them. The women have cried until no more tears will come. They have raged in anger and collapsed in despair. They have held each other and rocked like children. Now, as they walk toward the tomb, the women are silent. They are doing the only thing they know to do— going to the tomb. They are trying, somehow, to maintain contact with a man they loved beyond words. They are hoping to narrow the distance that death has set between them and Jesus. Something in them needs to confront the awful reality of his death, touch the grave and grieve.

Just as the tomb comes into view, the women are frightened by a powerful earthquake and a blinding light. They are shocked to see that the stone has been rolled away from the entrance. A figure bathed in light is sitting on the stone clothed in dazzling white. Even in their bewilderment, the women grasp that the figure is an angel. The guards are so frightened that they seem to be dead, yet something draws the women to the angel's presence. In contrast to the tremors of the earthquake, the angel's face is kind and the surrounding light—though brilliant—is warm and welcoming. A gentle, reassuring voice greets them: "Do not be afraid; I know that you are looking for Jesus who was crucified" (v. 5).

The women are dumbstruck—unnerved yet reassured. Their thoughts go immediately to Jesus. What's happening? Where's his body? The angel responds as though reading their thoughts: "He is not here; for he has been raised, as he said" (v. 6). The calm in the angel's voice encourages the women. In some strange way, it reminds them of what it was like to be in Jesus' presence. "Come," the angel continues, "see the place where he lay. Then go quickly and tell his disciples, 'He has been raised from the dead, and indeed is going ahead of you to Galilee; there you will see him.' This is my message for you" (vv. 6–7). As the women stare into the mysterious emptiness of the tomb, the Easter light begins to dawn in them. A sense of joy starts to counter their fear, and they find themselves running to deliver the angel's message.

Without warning, the women find themselves standing face-to-face with Jesus. Speechless, they stare at him in openmouthed disbelief. He is alive! Jesus greets them affectionately, and they collapse at his feet in a heap of jumbled emotions—fear…confusion…amazement…disbelief…joy. Shaking with both excitement and fear, they see the wounds in his feet. Yes, it's he! They embrace his feet in a gesture of surrender and worship.

Jesus' words reassure them: "Do not be afraid." Their eyes are fixed on him, but they are still unable to speak. A torrent of emotion washes over the women as energy and strength flow back into them. Feelings they thought they could never experience again begin to course through their veins. Their broken spirits soar as they encounter a possibility they never imagined.

All too soon, the moment passes. Jesus sends them forth with the same words the angel used. "Go and tell my brothers to go to Galilee; there they will see me" (v. 10). They long to stay in Jesus' presence, but his words and their desire to tell the disciples overwhelm them. They find themselves running—tears of joy streaming down their cheeks, laughing and frightened, unable to stop. As they run, the grief that had enveloped them melts into a fierce determination. A renewed vitality burns in their hearts. They find the strength to keep running even as their legs begin to ache and they have to fight for breath.

The women bang on the door where the disciples are staying, shouting to rouse them. When the door finally opens, the women are confronted by the disciples' frightened, bewildered looks. Gasping for breath, Mary Magdalene announces, "He's alive!" She senses the disciples' doubt and becomes even more adamant. "We saw him, he's alive." Chaos erupts. The women are breathless and ecstatic; the disciples, frightened and skeptical. Slowly, the women manage to relate their experiences—the earthquake, the stone, the angel, the empty tomb, their encounter with Jesus, his wounds. As all of them struggle to make sense of what is happening, the words of both Jesus and the angel give them direction: "...go to Galilee; there they will see me" (v. 10).

As we attempt to personalize the story of Jesus' resurrection, we are called to explore the transformational experiences in our own lives—those defining moments when dying gives way to new life and we are forever changed. As we explore the ways that the God of Easter takes us by surprise, we are called to trust the resurrection, embrace new life and tell others the story of our experiences.

How Does the Story Touch Me?

As I reflect on how the story of Jesus' resurrection touches my life, here are some of the ways that I connect with the experience of the story.

Surprised by New Life

The resurrection takes Mary Magdalene and the other Mary by surprise, and it overwhelms them. In the place of death they discover new life. As we attempt to personalize the story of Jesus' resurrection, we are called to explore the times when we have discovered new life in places of death.

As the women arrive at Jesus' tomb, they are greeted by the brilliant light of the resurrection. If I am honest with myself, I have to admit that there is something about that light that frightens me. When I encounter its sudden brightness, all too often my first instinct is to cling to the shadows or crawl under a rock. The unredeemed parts of me opt for the darkness. They prefer the moist earth of the tomb even if it leads to decay. The light of the resurrection reveals the doubts, fears and broken places within me that desperately need light yet resist its redemptive power.

The unredeemed parts of us tend to show up in places where they aren't invited. Late one evening I was packing to leave on an early morning flight. During the preceding days I had faced multiple deadlines, traveled too often and functioned on too little sleep. As I was putting things in my suitcase, I realized that I had forgotten to pick up an item at the store. I exploded, shouting a string of profanities at myself in a crescendo that culminated with "I am so stupid!" I had just settled back into the slow burn of silent anger when my wife, Carla, spoke. As gently as she could, she said, "Please don't say you're stupid because you're not." My response was to glare back at her, refusing to concede the point much less commit to reform. She is, of course, right. At times I do stupid things, but I am not stupid. At that moment, however, the unredeemed parts of me weren't buying it.

Over the next several days I reflected on what was behind my demeaning self-talk about being stupid. I recalled times when I was a kid doing chores with my dad—working on the car, repairing the house or tuning up the lawn mower. The memories are a bittersweet mixture of darkness and light. In particular I remembered that when I made a mistake or failed to carry out an instruction properly, he sometimes referred to me as "Sledgehead." I obviously never asked him to explain the reference, but I always assumed that it referred to the hardness of the forged steel in the head of a sledgehammer. The memory was a glimpse of the origins of the "I am so stupid" self-talk, a first step in reconnecting with some of the broken places inside me.

As I recalled these childhood memories, it was like climbing down a rope ladder into the darkness. I remembered an image that had come to me years before. In the image I am a young boy of nine or ten in my grandparents' home—a large old house with all kinds of nooks and crannies. I am sitting on the floor in the front closet hiding in the dark. I feel lost, alone and very sad. That image helped me uncover a broken part of me that had been entombed for years.

For several days I carried this image with me, reflecting on the feelings that accompanied it. I wasn't really trying to figure out the image, but I was aware of its presence. Slowly, I realized that part of me wanted to stay in the safety of that closet. Even tombs can be inviting. They may be dark, but at least they are familiar. Yet another part of me was longing for someone to come and open the door. That part of me was hoping to be redeemed, to be brought back into the light. At some point in reflecting on that image, a powerful insight dawned in me. The knob of the closet door was only inches from my face. I had control of whether I stayed in the darkness. Any time I chose to, I could open the door from the inside and walk into the light.

Sometimes the God of the resurrection comes to us in a blinding light and an angel's presence. Other times that same God comes to us in the realization that we are no longer ten years old, that we have a choice about whether we stay in the darkness and that we have within us the power to open the door and walk into the light. My negative self-talk had revealed broken places within me, and the image of the ten-year-old boy provided guidance for how to respond differently. For me the light of the resurrection dawned just as surely as it did for the women at Jesus' tomb. The difference was that that God knew me well enough to expose me to the light slowly, helping me learn to open the closet door a little bit each day.

A humorous sequel to my experience demonstrates how we can discover new life in the place of death. About a week after Carla chided me for calling myself "stupid," the two of us were in the kitchen fixing dinner. As she looked over a recipe she was preparing, she realized that she had left out an ingredient. Frustrated, she said to herself: "I'm such a dodo." The opportunity was just too good to pass up! After a dramatic pause, I assumed my best mock-seriousness and asked, "I just want to be sure that I understand the ground rules around here. Am I right that calling yourself 'a dodo' is acceptable, but saying 'I am so stupid' crosses the line?" There was an awkward silence, then she started laughing. "Yes," she replied, "you've pretty much got it." We both laughed—the laughter of surprise, the laughter of the women running from the tomb, the transforming laugh of Easter, the laughter that celebrates reconciliation and new life.

Overwhelmed by the Risen Christ

Mary Magdalene and the other Mary must have been overwhelmed by their face-to-face encounter with the Risen Jesus. They were expecting to anoint a corpse, but they found themselves in the presence of the glorified Christ. Although we don't have the experience of seeing the Risen Christ in his glorified body, personalizing this story invites us to explore the times when glimpses of the Risen Christ have overwhelmed us.

I had a glimpse of the Risen Christ on the December morning when I hit a patch of black ice driving sixty miles per hour. My car skidded off the road, hit a cement barrier, went airborne, rolled over several times and came to a stop on its roof. I crawled out of that tomb without a scratch. As I look back on it now, I realize that I know something of what Easter feels like. In that moment I experienced Christ's redeeming presence bringing life out of the places of death. I was overwhelmed by the experience of being spared.

We may get glimpses of the Risen Christ in the wonderful or the tragic. We may sense his presence in those experiences where life and death meet. We may recognize him when life has overpowered us and we are struggling to cope. We may find these experiences difficult to trust, even too personal to talk about. Yet in some hard-to-name way, we are aware of Christ's presence. When we experience the Risen Christ, we find ourselves struggling to get our bearings. A flood of emotions washes over us, and we are left dumbfounded—sometimes speechless, other times babbling. We shake our heads in disbelief, thinking it's too good to be true. We experience something like the earthquake that the women at Jesus' tomb endured, and the ground we're standing on shakes. The tremors vibrate through the beliefs that sustain us, and we have to struggle to keep our footing.

Every year I get a glimpse of the Risen Christ when I see the faces of those who emerge from the waters of baptism during the Easter Vigil. These men and women come to the baptismal font robed like monks. They take turns kneeling in the font with the water nearly waist-deep. The priest plunges each one face first into the water "in the name of the Father...," and then a second time: "and of the Son ...," and finally a third time: "...and of the Holy Spirit." As each of the newly baptized emerges from the font dripping from head to toe, the congregation greets its new member with a joyful song and heartwarming applause. Those being baptized are overwhelmed. Their faces express a unique mix of surprise, bewilderment, joy, relief and who knows what other emotions. They beam with an inner radiance as they receive the white robe of new life and the candle that represents the light of Christ.

The overwhelming part of the Easter Vigil is not just what happens to those being baptized; it's what happens to those of us who witness the event. As I watch those who have been transformed by baptism emerge from the water, I well up with tears of both joy and grief. Even though I have already taken the baptismal plunge, I am deeply aware of the many ways that I still need to be redeemed. The new life and profound joy of those being baptized reveal to me the ways that I resist the waters of life and cling instead to darkness and death. In spite of my baptism, the redemptive power of the water has yet to fully permeate my being. There is so much in me that still needs to be signed with the cross and washed in the waters of life. There is so much in me that still needs to die with Christ so that I can rise to new life in him.

The Easter Transformation

The experience of the Resurrection and the encounter with the Risen Christ leave the women profoundly changed. That experience is a defining moment, dividing their lives into "before" and "after." The Resurrection forces them to change their views of life and death and their beliefs about how God is present. Easter turns their lives upside down in some wonderful ways, including the discovery that Jesus is alive. Yet it also calls them beyond themselves to a frightening mission. As we personalize the story of Jesus' resurrection, we are invited to explore the defining moments in our own lives—those experiences that have called us to transformation. As we do so, we join the women in their struggle to let go of fear and trust the Resurrection. With them we discover the God of the Resurrection who turns our sorrow to joy and transforms our deaths into new life.

From Fear to Trust

Easter urges us to move beyond our fear and trust new life. There is no doubt that Easter frightens the women at the tomb. Both the angel and the Risen Jesus try to reassure them with the same words: "Do not be afraid" (vv. 5, 10). Like the women, our experience of the Easter transformation begins with fear.

My friend Nancy, an artist, once described her struggle with moving from fear to trust. She was taking a class to learn how to make printing plates. The process involves engraving a negative image into a metal plate with a sharp tool. When the finished plate is inked, it prints a positive image on paper. Nancy was in the studio working under the supervision of her teacher. She had been working on her plate for many hours, and she was trying to finish some of the intricate detail in the design. She had so much time invested in the plate that she was being very careful not to make a mistake. The teacher observed her tentative movements and said, "Nancy, you have to use great force on the plate or you'll never finish it." Instinctively, Nancy rebelled, exclaiming: "But, if I make a mistake, all my work will be ruined!" The teacher responded, "You have to trust that even if you make a mistake, you can rework the flaw into the beauty of a new design."

Easter calls us to trust a life-from-death God who helps us rework our flaws into the beauty of a new design. It urges us to leave the tombs, caves and closets of our fears behind and surrender to transformation. It urges us to embark on a journey to become our best and truest selves confident that the God of the resurrection is with us no matter what comes.

From Sorrow to Joy

Easter turns sorrow to joy. The women left the tomb filled with "great joy." The story reveals that joy is a defining characteristic of Easter people. Personalizing the story of Jesus' resurrection invites us to reflect on the measure of joy in our own lives.

As I consider the emotions that color my life, I'm forced to admit that there are times when my score on the "joy meter" comes up a little bit short. To be more candid about it, sometimes my attitude stinks. I have some positive traits, such as being generous. On the other side of the ledger, however, are my tendencies to be over-responsible and over-committing (I have difficulty with setting limits). So here's what happens. My modus operandi is to want to contribute, so I step forward to accept responsibility. Too often, however, I go too far and begin to lug around the weight of the world. I start thinking that I'm air traffic control for the universe. I get myself all worked up and walk around stoop-shouldered and grim-faced. If you've seen the cartoon where Ziggy is walking around with a storm cloud over his head, you get the idea.

There is more to Easter joy than some kind of magical mood swing from sad to happy. The joy of Easter is compelling because it is deeper than a "smiley-face" view of life that fails to grasp the ways that life is unfair, tragic and violent. Easter joy is not born in the shallow avoidance of life's dark places or the naïve inability to grasp the reality of evil. It is born in suffering, yet rooted in the conviction that death is not final. It dispels the notion that despair is our birthright by declaring that evil will not prevail. Easter joy is born at the tomb on the morning when the one who endured terrible suffering and a violent death rose victorious with coattails long enough to take all of us with him. Christian joy doesn't avoid what is painful and tragic. It endures it all, passes through and rises on the other side victorious.

My priest-friend Ken captures the essence of Easter joy. As a recovering alcoholic, he knows what it is to suffer. He has been to the bottom, fought transformation and lost. In fact, he lost big enough that he experienced something of Easter, rose again and claimed victory. That rising has given birth to an honesty that lets him talk about transformation in the first person. When he urges others to open themselves to transformation, he is able to talk about both the transformation that has taken place in him and his own continuing struggle to open himself to Easter. His experience of the Easter transformation from sorrow to joy also fuels an infectious enthusiasm that surprises people. As they pass him on the way into church on Sunday morning, he greets them with a smile and an alleluia. Then he asks, "Are you fired up yet?" Ken is the closest thing I know to a walking alleluia. It's not that he's always happy. As a priest he presides over life's tragedies as well as its joys. Like anyone who enters into the complexity of life, he has downs as well as ups. Yet what makes him a walking alleluia is his willingness to trust that the Easter transformation will overcome all. He is a walking alleluia because he is willing to let the joy of Easter shine through him undiminished. Even when Ken goes down into the depths of the tomb, he trusts that God will raise him up and transform his sorrow into an enduring alleluia.

FROM DEATH TO NEW LIFE

Easter brings new life out of death. We experience death in the loss of a job, the ending of a relationship, the failure to reach a lifelong goal or the passing of a loved one. As we personalize the passage from death to life, we search our experiences of death to discover the God of life.

One Thanksgiving I experienced a painful inner death. At the time my stepchildren were teenagers. Carla and I wanted to make the family's Thanksgiving meal prayer more meaningful, so we decided to encourage each person at the table to give thanks for something specific. Carla and I agreed that I would explain the prayer and then begin the litany of thanks. I had led similar prayers on any number of occasions, but never with my family. Something in the intimacy of the experience triggered unexpected emotions.

Before I could get half a sentence out, the words stuck in my throat. I became totally incoherent, and I felt extremely vulnerable. My eyes filled with tears, and I couldn't continue. I sat there in a terrible silence, struggling to regain my composure. Finally, after what seemed like an eternity, I was forced to give up. I motioned to the person sitting next to me to continue and slumped down in my chair completely humiliated.

As I sat there dying, something amazing happened. Each person at the table began to share prayers of gratitude. Soon the litany of thanks to God and to each other was flowing freely. One of my stepdaughters had been fighting with her mother and me for several days. She concluded her prayer by thanking God for "semi-reasonable parents." I was stunned. The God of Easter had brought new life out of death. Something in me had died, but something wonderful rose from the ashes to transform those of us gathered at the table.

There are many ways we pass from death to life. We experience the Easter transformation whenever we extend ourselves on behalf of someone else. We experience it when we keep our egos in check to make room for the growth and change that love requires. We experience it whenever we devote our lives to something greater than we are, whether we pour ourselves out a little bit each day for years or give ourselves once and for all in a moment of total sacrifice. In all these deaths the God of resurrection is with us as surely as that Thanksgiving when I was struck dumb to clear the way for new life.

An image came to me as I was writing this chapter. In the image I am with my father and my older brother—both of whom died years ago. We are walking down a dark tunnel toward a bright light. Having read Raymond Moody's book *Life After Life*,[1] I immediately recognized this as an image of dying. Moody interviewed over a hundred people who had experienced clinical death and been brought back to life. They described going through a dark tunnel toward a bright light. In the image, my father and brother are beside me. Someday, like them, I will pass through that tunnel. It is the inevitable passage every human being makes. The image has two powerful elements. Death is the dark tunnel. A light draws us through the tunnel. Those of us who are Christian know that light as Christ. He has been raised and has gone before us to prepare the way. The Christ light draws us through the tunnel of death and welcomes us home. My father and my brother have already made that journey. Someday I will make that passage and so will you. The light of the resurrection that dawned on Easter calls us home and guides us there. It is the porch light that we walk toward no matter how lost and alone we feel. Ultimately, we will experience that light as the warm and welcoming presence of Christ guiding us to our eternal home and folding us in an endless embrace.

Go and Tell

In this story of Jesus' resurrection, both the angel and Jesus give Mary Magdalene and her friend Mary the mission to "go and tell." Those who experience Easter are sent to spread the news. As we personalize the story of Jesus' resurrection, we are invited to reflect on our own call to "go and tell."

Earlier in this chapter I described the glimpse of the Risen Christ that I see in the faces of those who are baptized during the Easter Vigil. The Rite of Christian Initiation of Adults that prepares them to receive baptism and the other sacraments of initiation is a direct expression of the great commission. Baptism is an immersion in Jesus' passage from death to life. It is a definitive expression of Christian identity—dying with Christ so that we may rise with him. In baptism we celebrate our own passage from death to life and receive the same commission as the women on Easter morning and the disciples on the mountain in Galilee: "Go and tell."

In the weeks following the Easter Vigil, my parish encourages the newly baptized to "go and tell" by inviting them to share their stories of faith with the entire community. These stories are intensely personal and richly varied. Yet I have also been struck by the common themes that surface again and again. The themes are wonderful expressions of the passage from death to new life. Here is a sample of them in the words of those recently baptized.

- "I knew there was something missing in my life, but I didn't know what it was."
- "I went through a time of searching and questioning."
- "For a long time, I felt lost and alone."
- "I met someone in the parish who welcomed and accepted me."
- "I decided to explore becoming a part of this community."
- "I began to recognize ways that God is a part of my life and has been for a long time."
- "I opened myself to God, and I made faith more a part of my life."
- "I saw that there were things in my life that needed to change."
- "I struggled to overcome destructive behaviors in my life."
- "I found that God gave me the strength to change and live in a different way."
- "More and more, I found myself able to let go and trust God."
- "I decided to surrender to God, and I chose to be baptized (or make a profession of faith)."
- "Through it all—even the difficult times—I discovered a sense of joy and peace."
- "I know that my journey isn't over; it will continue for the rest of my life."
- "I'm so grateful for what I've gained that I want to share it with others."
- "I hope that I have the opportunity to reach out to others and encourage them on their journeys of faith."

Each story describes personal experiences of God's redeeming presence. The newly baptized express in vivid detail how they have been touched and changed by an Easter God. The themes that emerge from their stories are a powerful demonstration of the passage from death to life.

As I've listened to these stories over the years, it has become clear to me that people emerge from the waters of baptism with a strong desire to "go and tell." They endure the discomfort of standing in front of hundreds of people to tell their stories because they have a deep need to share the good news of their passage from death to life. It is not that these people are likely to find speaking to large groups the usual venue for sharing their faith. This experience, however, gives them a taste of what it means to "go and tell."

The enthusiasm of the newly baptized to "go and tell" is in sharp contrast with my own reluctance to share my story of faith. I hesitate to share it with my closest friends, to say nothing of strangers and crowds. Listening to the stories of how the newly baptized have come to faith is both a wake-up call for me and a challenge to the entire community to renew our commitment to "go and tell."

When people experience something wonderful, they spontaneously share it with others. It's unimaginable that Mary Magdalene and her friend Mary could have encountered the Risen Jesus and then gone on about their daily routine. Whether or not Jesus gave them the mission to "go and tell," they had to tell others.

The night that Mark proposed to Tracy and she said "yes" was a night of celebration. They shared wonderful time as a couple. Then, no longer able to contain their joy, they had to go and tell. They started making phone calls to family and friends until the rejoicing had spread from New Jersey to Oregon. That's what happens when something wonderful occurs; we bubble over and tell others.

The people who emerge from the waters of baptism at the Easter Vigil are experiencing a high point on their journey of faith. The Rite of Christian Initiation of Adults has brought them to this moment alive and aware. Their faith life is vibrant and new. Like Mark and Tracy, they can't keep the news to themselves. They have a story to tell, and their enthusiasm overpowers their reluctance. They go for it and tell their stories.

How Does This Story Call Me to Live?

As you try to make the story of Jesus' resurrection a part of your life, here are some questions to live and a suggestion for prayer.

Living the Questions

One or more of the following questions may help you live the story of Jesus' resurrection more fully.

- As I reflect on the story of Jesus' resurrection, what experiences in my own life help me connect with the story?

- What are some of the defining moments in my own life—those experiences in which I was surprised to discover new life in a place of death?

- To what extent is my life characterized by Easter joy?

- What themes that the newly baptized describe in their journey of faith (pp. 107–108) resonate with my own journey of faith?

- In what way have I experienced the call to "go and tell"? How have I responded to that call?

Entering Into Prayer

Reflecting on the story of Jesus' resurrection led me to this Easter prayer:

Easter Prayer

Life-giving God of Easter, you continue to surprise your disciples with dazzling light and empty tombs. Shine the light of

Christ into the unredeemed places within me. You know all of my doubts, fears and broken places. You are aware of the ways I resist light and hide in the darkness. Be relentless in pursuing me with the light of Christ. Give me the courage to open the doors I hide behind. Roll back every stone in my life and help me walk into the light. Alleluia!

Life-giving God of Easter, you overwhelmed the women at the tomb with their unexpected encounter with the Risen Christ. When I am overwhelmed by either the wonderful or the tragic, help me to recognize the presence of the Risen Christ. When life overpowers me and I am struggling to cope, give me a deep sense of your presence. Help me to open my life to you so that Easter takes deep root in my spirit. Let my whole life prepare me for the divine ambush when I will meet you face to face. Alleluia!

Life-giving God of Easter, transform my fear into trust. You know the ways that fear diminishes me, triggering my defenses and causing knee-jerk reactions. Open my heart to the Easter message of "Do not be afraid." Help me to trust that you are with me, bringing life out of death and reworking my flaws into the beauty of a new design. Give me the courage to embark on the journey of trust to become my best and truest self. Give me a deep and abiding confidence that you are with me always no matter what comes. Alleluia!

Life-giving God of Easter, turn my sorrow into joy. You know every emotion and mood that colors my life. You know when I have a bad attitude and how seldom my life is characterized by joy. When I walk around grim-faced and stoop-shouldered, remind me that Easter has the power to weave sunshine out of rain.[2] Let the pain and suffering that I endure give way to the profound joy of Easter. Let it seize my heart and overflow on all those I meet. Alleluia!

Life-giving God of Easter, bring new life out of my experiences of death. You know how fiercely I resist dying and cling instead to my selfish attempts to get my own way. Give me the courage to surrender to the power of Easter. Help me trust that you are with me to bring new life out of the ways that I die to myself every day. Prepare me for the day that you call me through the dark tunnel of death so that I am ready to embrace the light of Christ. Alleluia!

Life-giving God of Easter, empower me for my mission to "go and tell." You know my reluctance to tell my story of faith. Be with me when I swallow hard and wish that I could find some place to hide. In those moments give me the courage to overcome my reluctance to share my story of faith. Give me the courage to trust that, even if I begin my story in a halting and uncertain way, you will be with me to conclude it with the spontaneous shout that defines Easter joy. Alleluia!

CHAPTER EIGHT

A GUIDE TO PERSONALIZING GOSPEL STORIES

Each story chapter in this book is the result of my attempt to personalize a Gospel story. The purpose of this chapter is to explain a method you can use to deepen your own ability to personalize stories in the Scriptures.

The goal of personalizing a Gospel story is to unlock the power of God's word and deepen your relationship with the incarnate God that embraces us in Jesus Christ. The approach I use to personalizing each story has four steps:

- Opening myself to the story
- Entering into the experience of the story
- Making connections between the story and my own life
- Living out the story

As you consider the specific techniques suggested in this chapter, keep in mind that the beauty and uniqueness of a relationship—particularly your relationship with God—can't be reduced to a method or a set of techniques. What makes relationships so wonderful is that they are vibrant, dynamic and unpredictable. Think of these techniques as a place to start, but remember that your ultimate goal is to enter into the story and deepen your relationship with God.

Some of the techniques may open new doors for you while others may leave you cold. Use the ones that are helpful and have the courage to invent others that are unique to you. If you find yourself getting stuck, be patient. Remember, you're not the only one working on this relationship. Trust that an ever-faithful God will come to you at the appropriate time in a unique and perhaps surprising way.

OPENING MYSELF TO THE STORY

Being open to a Gospel story begins with readiness. I get ready by quieting myself, trying to let go of distractions, and focusing my energy and attention on the story.

Part of this process is a quieting prayer.

Quieting Prayer

A quieting prayer is a simple prayer asking God for help in focusing on the story and opening my heart to it. I invite God to speak to me through the story. Much of my life is lived at high speed in a noisy world, and I need to let go of that in order to be ready to listen.

For me, this type of prayer usually involves sitting quietly, breathing slowly and deeply, and asking for help in letting go of my worries and preoccupations. I ask God to open me to the story. Sometimes I use my journal to focus my attention on the here and now. Other times I pray a favorite psalm or Scripture passage, such as Psalm 23, Psalm 25 or Psalm 139. Occasionally, I use a more formal quieting prayer.

Here is an example of such a prayer. Try praying it and see if it leads you to discover a quieting prayer of your own.

"To you, O God, I lift up my soul. In you, O my God, I trust."
(Psalm 25:1–2)

Great God, my world is spinning too fast. Sometimes I love the pace and let myself get caught up in it. Other times it leaves me dizzy, confused and exhausted.

Slow me down, O God. I want to spend a few minutes with you that will be different, and I need your help.

Help me breathe deeply,

quiet myself

and turn toward you.

Help me give you my full attention,

listen with an open heart

and trust in your word.

"To you, O God, I lift up my soul. In you, O my God, I trust."

My mind is so easily distracted by my list of things to do. Help me be quiet and focus my mind, my heart and my whole self on you.

My heart is hungry and filled with longing. Help me focus that hunger and longing on you.

My spirit is restless. Help me bring my restlessness to you and receive your gift of peace.

"To you, O God, I lift up my soul. In you, O my God, I trust."

For the next few minutes help me open myself to your word.

Let it touch me deeply,

draw me closer to you,

call me to conversion, and

give me the courage to live for you.

"To you, O God, I lift up my soul. In you, O my God, I trust."

Great God, I am aware that part of me is afraid of taking this time,

afraid of opening my heart to you,

afraid of what you may ask of me,

afraid of what your call may demand of me.

Give me the courage to face that fear,

help me listen even when I am afraid, and

help me trust that you love the part of me that is frightened as deeply as you love the part of me that has the courage to risk opening my heart.

"To you, O God, I lift up my soul. In you, O my God, I trust."

Wonderful Creator, help me turn my attention toward you.

Merciful Redeemer, gift me with an open heart.

Spirit of Love, give me the courage to move beyond fear to trust.

Help me make these few minutes a gift to you.

I will try to gift you with them even when I am distracted and afraid.

Touch me with the power of your word so that it may gift me with light and life.

"To you, O God, I lift up my soul. In you, O my God, I trust."

Great and wonderful God,

be with me as I try to take this story to heart.

Help me be open to the experience of the story, and

let it touch the depths of my spirit and come to life in me.

"To you, O God, I lift up my soul. In you, O my God, I trust."

ENTERING INTO THE EXPERIENCE OF THE STORY

After praying a quieting prayer, I am ready to enter into the experience of the story. Here are three techniques I use to immerse myself in it.

Slow Reading of the Story

The first technique is slow reading. I read the story as slowly as possible—as though I am savoring the taste of a good wine or lingering over my favorite dessert. I may read it over slowly three, four, five times or more. At first I just want to appreciate it as a story. Then, as I continue to read and re-read it, I try to pay attention to every detail.

As I am doing this slow reading, some of the questions that I keep in mind include:

- What's the conflict in the story? What's at stake, and how does this conflict play out?

- Who's involved in the story? What is each person feeling, and how does the conflict impact each one?
- As the story unfolds, what surprises or intrigues me?

There are additional ways of using slow reading to enter into the story. In discussing his novella *Shopgirl* on *The Today Show*, writer and actor Steve Martin described the way he reads his stories aloud to get a deeper appreciation of the impact of the words.[1] The Gospel stories grew out of an oral tradition. Long before they were written down, these stories were told aloud. Reading them aloud may help you experience them in a new way.

The late Bishop Ken Untener often memorized Gospel stories word-for-word. Memorization requires both repetition and paying careful attention to each word and phrase. Both lead to a deeper experience of the story. For Bishop Untener the discipline of memorization also let him proclaim the Gospel without looking at the lectionary. As a result, the story came to life in him, and his listeners experienced it in a new way.

When I am trying to personalize a Gospel story, I like to read it every morning and "take it with me" through the day. By doing this, I am able to live with the story for a while. This way of spending time with the story day after day helps me open myself to it and discover connections with my own life.

If you are reading this book during the weeks of Lent, try personalizing the appropriate Gospel story each week. Begin personalizing the story on the Monday before it will be proclaimed during worship the following weekend. Spend time with the story each day, seeing the ways that it connects with your own experience. By opening yourself to the story in this way, you will be prepared to experience it in a new and deeper way when it is proclaimed to the community during the weekend liturgy.

Taking Verse-by-Verse Notes

As I slowly read and reread the story, I find it helpful to take notes on verses that capture my attention. I like to jot down key words or phrases that seem significant to the experience of the story. These notes often include:

- Aspects of the story that surprise me
- The questions I have about what certain verses mean
- Intriguing details of the story that capture my attention

In my verse-by-verse review of the story, I pay particular attention to several elements:

- Spoken words and quotes often provide important clues to the story's meaning.
- Words that express feeling or emotion help me grasp the experience of the people in the story.
- Questions the story poses are often the questions I need to wrestle with as I personalize the story.

Noting the significance of these elements in the story helps me enter more deeply into the experience of the story.

Identifying With the Emotion of a Particular Person

Entering into any story, including a Gospel story, is experiential. We are touched by the emotion of the story, and we are moved. The power of a great book is that it engages our emotions and becomes our story. It captures our imagination, and we begin to actually live the story.

As I attempt to enter into the experience of a Gospel story, I often choose a particular person in the story and try to identify with that person's experience. In chapter two I identified with both the awe and bewilderment of the three disciples who experienced Jesus' Transfiguration (Matthew 17:1–13). In chapter four I identified with the healing and transformation of the man born blind (John 9:1–41). In chapter six I identified with the disciples who abandoned Jesus and with the way Simon of Cyrene was forced to help Jesus carry his cross (Matthew 26:14—27:66).

Once I choose a person, I try to "get inside that person's skin." I want to live the story from his or her perspective—seeing what the person saw, feeling what the person felt. This emotional identification with a specific person gets me out of my head and into my gut. I am no longer thinking about the story, I am feeling it. Immersing myself in the experience of a specific person helps me to grasp the story at a deeper, more emotional level.

To enter more deeply into the story, I usually go from one person in the story to another—identifying with the experience of each. This helps me grasp the conflict in the story in a deeper way, and I come to appreciate the many perspectives in the story. Identifying with the emotions of people on both sides of a conflict helps me to see how the conflict in the story is a mirror for my own inner conflict. It helps me see that I face the same feelings, choices and consequences that the people in the story face.

For an example of how emotional identification with more than one person in the story helps unlock the experience of the story, review chapter five. In that chapter I used emotional identification to get in touch with both the similarities and the contrasts between Lazarus's two grieving sisters—Martha and Mary. I also used it to identify with the messenger who was dispatched to Jesus, the people in the crowd who witnessed the miracle, Jesus and even Lazarus. This multidimensional approach helped me grasp the emotional power of the story.

I find that identifying with the emotions of Jesus is particularly helpful in more fully appreciating his humanness. It helps me feel what he felt and imagine what he might have thought in each situation. This serves to deepen my relationship with him and is a way of entering into prayer.

MAKING CONNECTIONS WITH MY LIFE

By entering into the experience of the story, I begin to make connections with experiences in my own life that are similar to those of the people in the story. As a result, I begin to see God's presence in my own life in new and deeper ways. Here are three techniques that I find helpful in making and deepening those connections.

Recognizing Similar Experiences in My Own Life

The process of making connections is more experiential than logical. The key question to ask is: When have I had an experience similar to this story? At the heart of making these connections is recognizing the way in which the Gospel story is my story too.

Here some examples from other chapters of the book to illustrate how the various Gospel stories helped me make connections with my own life.

- As I reflected on how the Spirit led Jesus into the desert and his experience of loneliness and temptation, I came to recognize more deeply how moving to San Francisco was a "desert experience" in my own life (chapter one).

- As I entered into the pain of the Samaritan woman's broken relationships and her longing for a love that will last, I connected with both my own longing and my experience of abandonment in two very different love relationships (chapter three).

- As I touched the grief and loss that Martha and Mary felt when Lazarus died, I connected with the grief and loss that I experienced when my brother was killed in a plane crash (chapter five).

The key to connecting a story in the Gospels with my own experience is being willing to risk vulnerability. Taking the story to heart goes far deeper than a mental exercise. It requires that I embrace all the pathos in the story and expose myself to its conflicts, emotions and struggles. When we let a story touch our hearts in this deeply personal way, it invites us on the ultimate spiritual adventure: being touched and changed by the presence of God. Once we set off on that adventure, there's no telling where it will lead.

Asking Core Questions to Make the Connection

Sometimes I find that it's quite difficult to make connections between the Gospel story and my own life. Even after taking time to reflect on the story, I may find myself coming up empty. When that happens, I find it helpful to reflect on one or more core questions to try to see the story in a new way.

- How does this story touch me?
- In what way is this story "good news" for me?
- In what way does the story affirm me and make me stronger?
- In what way does the story challenge me and call me to change?
- How does the story call me to live?
- If I take this story to heart, how would my life be different?
- What's one thing I can do today to let this story live in me?

Patience is also an important discipline in making connections between the Gospel story and my own life. Some connections come quickly: I recognized that moving to San Francisco was a desert experience for me (chapter one) within a few minutes. Other connections are slower and more painful. It took me weeks to grasp the dynamics of Jesus' passion and the ways in which I connected with that experience (chapter six). It may take you that much time, or even much longer.

There is no reason to rush the personalization process or try to force quick connections. Unlike most things in life, personalization has no deadlines or time limits. Sometimes the story has to simmer on the back burner for days before its power connects with our lives. Don't worry or hurry. Trust that you will be graced with the ability to recognize these connections in God's good time.

Deepening the Connection

Making connections between a Gospel story and my own life is powerful in and of itself. To fully appreciate God's presence in our lives, however, we need to reflect more deeply on that connection. I find it helpful to use writing as a tool for deepening this connection, and this book is evidence of that.

Sometimes I write in my journal to reflect on the ways that some aspect of the Gospel story is either similar to or different from my own experience. At other times I use a more concise approach to writing. I divide a sheet of paper into two columns. In the left column I list characteristics of the Gospel story. In the right column I list characteristics in my own life that are either similar to or different from those in the left column. This process usually leads me to finding deeper connections than I first realized.

It's up to you whether you choose journal writing, the more structured "two-column approach" or just reflect informally on these connections. The main thing is to recognize that you need time and reflection to deepen your appreciation of how the Gospel story connects with your own life. Only then will you be able to mine the rich vein of spiritual insight that the story conveys and fully recognize how God is present in your own experience.

LIVING OUT THE STORY

Personalizing a Gospel story goes beyond recognizing the connections between the story and our own lives. We are called to live the story, internalize its significance and make it a vital part of our lives. As the story begins to live in us, the Jesus touch who changed the lives of the people in the story begins to transform us.

Here are two ways that I try to make each Gospel story a part of my life, to "take it with me" on my life journey.

Living the Questions That Emerge From the Story

As the *Living the Questions* section of each chapter in this book demonstrates, the process of personalizing a Gospel story leads me to formulate questions about the implications of the story for my own life. Here are some examples:

• The story of Jesus' encounter with the woman at the well (chapter three) led me to ask myself the question: What is my deepest thirst?

• The story of the man born blind (chapter four) helped me ask myself in what way I needed and longed for Jesus' healing touch.

• The story of Jesus disappointing Mary and Martha by not arriving before Lazarus died (chapter five) urged me to ask myself when God had disappointed me by failing to show up in time.

I find that these questions become powerful ways to carry the story with me throughout the day and week. As I ponder such questions, the story's impact on me grows. It is a subtle process that takes time—like giving a cup of tea time to steep in order to bring out its full flavor.

There is no need to formulate a lot of questions. The important thing is to find one that has particular meaning for you and carry it with you. As you do so, this question will help the story grow in you. It will guide you in making the story a deeper part of your life.

Entering Into Prayer

A second way that the story becomes a part of my life is illustrated by the *Entering Into Prayer* section of each chapter. As my awareness of the meaning and impact of a story grows, it naturally leads me to prayer. My deeper grasp of how God is present in my life fosters a sense of gratitude that I express as praise and thanks.

Although each chapter of this book contains suggestions for entering into prayer, authentic prayer is deeply personal. As you enter into each story, trust that the prayer you need to pray will emerge spontaneously from deep within you. If no words come, let the silence be your prayer. Trust that this prayerful surrender is a place where you will encounter the God who longs to be a part of your life.

A Concluding Thought

This chapter suggests an approach for personalizing stories in the Scriptures and some techniques that you may find helpful. Ultimately, the goal of personalizing these stories is to enter more deeply into relationship with God and unlock the power of God's word. Achieving this goal is more about engagement and surrender than it is about approach or technique. There is no one way. I have explained some of what I have learned to give you a place to start. As you embark on this journey, you will discover ways that are uniquely your own. If you take the first few steps, you'll find it's a marvelous journey...

NOTES

Chapter One: Claiming Our True Identity
Jesus Is Tempted in the Desert

1. Henri J.M. Nouwen, *With Open Hands* (Notre Dame, Ind.: Ave Maria Press, 1995).

2. I remember this quote from an issue of *MAD Magazine* I read years ago. I have been unable to locate the original citation.

3. John K. Ryan, trans. *The Confessions of St. Augustine* (New York: Image Books/Doubleday & Company, 1960), p. 43.

4. *The Birdcage*, Copyright ©1996, MGM Home Entertainment, United Artists Pictures.

Chapter Two: Glimpses of God Touching Us
The Transfiguration of Jesus

1. I first heard the "God touching you" question from Father John Gallen, S.J., when he was the director of the Notre Dame Center for Pastoral Liturgy at the University of Notre Dame.

2. Anthony Quinn, *The Original Sin* (Boston: Little, Brown, and Company, 1972).

3. Quinn, p. 111.

4. Henri J.M. Nouwen, *Life of the Beloved: Spiritual Living in a Secular World* (New York: The Crossroad Publishing Company, 1996).

5. Nouwen, p. 26.

6. Donald P. McNeil, Douglas A. Morrison and Henri J.M. Nouwen, *Compassion: A Reflection on the Christian Life* (New York: Doubleday & Company, 1982), p. 89.

7. As I recall, this is the title of Father Mike Kolar's presentation. To the best of my knowledge, it was never published.

Chapter Three: Acknowledging Our Deeper Thirst
Jesus Meets the Woman at the Well

1. *The Big Chill*, Copyright ©1983, Columbia Pictures Industries, Inc.

2. Edna St. Vincent Millay, Amy Shapiro, ed. *A Woman's Notebook: Being a Blank Book with Quotes by Women* (Philadelphia: Running Press, 1980).

Chapter Four: Opening Ourselves to the Jesus Touch
Jesus Heals the Man Born Blind

1. Antoine de Saint-Exupéry, Richard Howard, trans. *The Little Prince* (New York: Harcourt, Inc. 1943), p. 63.

2. Visit timjmcguire.com for more information about Tim, his columns and his other activities.

Chapter Five: Confronting Stagnation and Death
Jesus Raises Lazarus From the Dead

1. *Papillon*, Copyright ©1973, Columbia Pictures Industries, Inc.

Chapter Six: A Love Stronger Than Death
Jesus' Passion and Death

1. *Saving Private Ryan*, Copyright ©1998, DreamWorks SKG.

2. M. Scott Peck, *The Different Drum: Community Making and Peace* (New York: Touchstone, Simon and Schuster Inc., 1988).

3. Victor Hugo, Lee Fahnestock and Norman MacAfee, trans. *Les Miserables* (New York: Signet Classic, 1987).

4. Henry David Thoreau, *Walden and Other Writings* (New York: Modern Library, 2000), p. 72.

5. At the time of the crash of Air Florida Flight 90, the heroic sacrifice of Arland D. Williams, Jr., was widely reported. An example of

that coverage is "A Hero—Passenger Aids Others, Then Dies," *The Washington Post*, January 14, 1982.

Chapter Seven: Surprised by the God of Easter
Jesus Is Raised From the Dead

1. Raymond A. Moody, Jr., *Life After Life: The Investigation of a Phenomenon—Survival of Bodily Death* (San Francisco: HarperSanFrancisco, 2001).

2. The phrase "weave sunshine out of rain" is based on the song "Weave Me the Sunshine" by Peter Yarrow, Copyright ©1972, Mary-Beth Music—ASCAP.

Chapter Eight: A Guide to Personalizing Gospel Stories

1. Steve Martin, *Shopgirl* (New York: Theia, A Division of Hyperion, 2000).

ANNOTATED BIBLIOGRAPHY

This bibliography describes book categories that will help you deepen your ability to personalize the Gospel. It also suggests several titles in each category that you may find helpful.

INTRODUCTIONS TO THE BIBLE

A number of books are available to introduce you to the Bible and specific books of the Bible. These works will help you understand the meaning and context of biblical stories so that you can more effectively grasp their meaning in your own life.

Here are three general introductions. The thematic approach of Martos and Rohr encourages personalizing the Scriptures. Brown's work will appeal to those who want a more scholarly approach.

Brueggemann, Walter. *The Bible Makes Sense.* Cincinnati: St. Anthony Messenger Press, 2003.

Brown, Raymond E. *Introduction to the New Testament by Raymond E. Brown.* New York: Doubleday, 1997.

Martos, Joseph and Richard Rohr. *The Great Themes of Scripture: New Testament.* Cincinnati: St. Anthony Messenger Press, 1988.

Martos, Joseph and Richard Rohr. *The Great Themes of Scripture: Old Testament.* Cincinnati: St. Anthony Messenger Press, 1987.

Here are introductions to the two Gospels, Matthew and John, which are the sources for the stories in this book.

Apicella, Raymond. *Journeys Into Matthew: 18 Lessons of Exploration and Discovery.* Cincinnati: St. Anthony Messenger Press, 1996.

Brown, Raymond E. *Introduction to the Gospel of John by Raymond E. Brown.* New York: Doubleday, 1997.

In addition to the above introductions, here is a convenient compilation of the Sunday readings throughout the three years of the liturgical calendar.

Sunday's Word: Year A. Chicago: GIA, 2004. There are also volumes with the same title for Year B and Year C of the liturgical calendar.

CHRISTIAN AUTOBIOGRAPHY

Christian autobiography flows from the bold belief that "my story" is really "the story of how God touches me." This notion is at the heart of personalizing the Gospels, and here are three examples. Augustine's *Confessions* gave birth to this genre, Merton's autobiography is a modern classic, and Lamott's memoir is a unique contemporary contribution.

Lamott, Anne. *Traveling Mercies: Some Thoughts on Faith.* New York: Anchor, 1999.

Merton, Thomas. *The Seven Storey Mountain.* New York: Harcourt Brace, 1948.

Ryan, John K., trans. *The Confessions of St. Augustine.* New York: Image, 1960.

BOOKS ON STORY

Here are two interesting examples of using story to more deeply understand the Scriptures. Sanford's unique approach uses psychological insight to bring biblical characters to life. Shea is one of the best contemporary Christian storytellers.

Sanford, John. *The Man Who Wrestled With God: Light from the Old Testament on the Psychology of Individuation.* Mahwah, N.J.: Paulist, 1981.

Shea, John. *Stories of God: An Unauthorized Biography.* Notre Dame, Ind.: Ave Maria, 1996.

PREACHING AND LISTENING TO THE WORD

If you want help preaching, teaching and hearing the Word as it is proclaimed during worship, here are three suggestions.

Faley, Roland J. *Footprints on the Mountain: Preaching and Teaching the Sunday Readings.* Mahwah, N.J.: Paulist, 1994.

Knight, David. *Living God's Word: Reflections on the Weekly Gospels— Years A, B and C.* Cincinnati: St. Anthony Messenger Press, 1998.

Pilch, John. *The Cultural World of the Jesus: Sunday by Sunday—Cycles A, B and C.* Collegeville, Minn.: The Liturgical Press, 1995.

PRAYING THE BIBLE

Here are three suggestions for using the stories in Scripture to deepen your prayer.

Nouwen, Henri J.M. *With Open Hands.* Notre Dame, Ind.: Ave Maria, 1995.

Rosage, David. *Speak, Lord, Your Servant Is Listening.* Cincinnati: Servant Books, 1987.

Zyromski, Page McKean. *Pray the Bible.* Cincinnati: St. Anthony Messenger Press, 2000.

POETRY

Personalizing the gospel requires slowing down and paying careful attention—which is a unique gift of poets and something we can learn from them. Here's a suggested title for two of my favorite contemporary poets.

Oliver, Mary. *House of Light*. Boston: Beacon, 1990.

Whyte, David. *Everything Is Waiting for You*. Langley, Wash.: Many Rivers, 2003.